MODERN LITERATURE MONOGRAPHS

GENERAL EDITOR: Lina Mainiero

(continued on last page of book)

RING LARDNER

Elizabeth Evans

FREDERICK UNGAR PUBLISHING CO.
NEW YORK

Library of Congress Cataloging in Publication Data

Evans, Elizabeth, 1935–
  Ring Lardner.

  (Modern literature monographs)
  Bibliography: p.
  Includes index.
  1. Lardner, Ring Wilmer, 1885–1933—Criticism and
interpretation.

PS3523.A7Z655   818′.5′209 [B]   79-4829
ISBN 0-8044-2185-4

Contents

Chronology

1885	March 6, Ringgold Wilmer Lardner is born in Niles, Michigan, to wealthy parents, Henry and Lena Phillips Lardner. He was the youngest of nine children and was always called Ring.
1890–1901	Educated at home and at Niles High School where he graduated in 1901.
1901	Family suffers financial setback. Works briefly at various jobs.
1902	Goes to Armour Institute in Chicago in an unsuccessful attempt to study engineering.
1903–05	Works for the Niles Gas Company in various capacities in Niles, participates in productions of the Niles American Minstrel group, writes music and most of lyrics for a two-act musical comedy, *Zanzibar*.
1905–07	Begins his newspaper career on the South Bend, Indiana, *Times*.
1907–08	Moves to Chicago and is reporter first for the Chicago *Inter-Ocean,* then the Chicago *Examiner*. Assigned to travel on the spring tour with the Chicago White Sox. Covers their games that season.
1908–10	Baseball reporter for the Chicago *Tribune*.

1910–11   After leaving the *Tribune,* Lardner works briefly as managing editor and feature writer for the St. Louis *Sporting News,* as sports editor for the Boston *American,* and later as copyreader for the Chicago *American.*

1911   Marries Ellis Abbott on June 28.

1912   Baseball writer for Chicago *Examiner.* A son, John Abbott, is born on May 4.

1913   Writes the prestigious daily variety column, "In the Wake of the News" for the Chicago *Tribune.* He continues in this capacity for six years.

1914   Ten stories in the *Saturday Evening Post* about Jack Keefe, semi-literate bush league pitcher, begin his career as a fiction writer. With Edward C. Heeman, he brings out a souvenir booklet, *The Homecoming of Charles A. Comiskey, James J. Callahan and John J. McGraw,* celebrating the return of the Chicago White Sox and the New York Giants from their 1914 world tour. James Phillips, born May 18.

1915   Ringgold Wilmer, Jr., his third son, born August 19. Called Bill.

1917   Sequence of stories about the Gullibles collected and published as *Gullible's Travels.* Collier's sends him to France for a brief trip as a war correspondent.

1918   Publishes *Treat 'Em Rough,* Jack Keefe's war adventures.

1919   Publishes *You Know Me Al, The Real Dope* and *Own Your Own Home.* Left the *Tribune* and moved with his family to Greenwich, Connecticut. Began writing a "Weekly Letter" for the Bell Syndicate.

	David Ellis, his fourth son, born March 11.
1920	Publishes *The Young Immigrunts*.
1921	Publishes *The Big Town,* four collected stories that had appeared the previous year. Moved to Great Neck, Long Island, to The Mange. Published *Symptoms of Being 35.*
1923–24	Wrote text for Bell Syndicate comic strip based on *You Know Me Al* from October 1923 to fall 1924.
1924	Turning point in his career came with publication of *How To Write Short Stories.*
1925	Scribner's publishes *What of It?* and reissued in a uniform edition *You Know Me Al, Gullible's Travels,* and *The Big Town.*
1926	Publishes *The Love Nest and Other Stories.*
1927	Publishes *The Story of Wonder Man.* Tuberculosis diagnosed. Stops writing "Weekly Letter" to devote more time to theatrical ventures.
1928	Moved to East Hampton, Long Island, his last home. *Elmer, the Great,* a play with George M. Cohan, failed. Brief journalistic writing for the *Telegraph* brought needed income.
1929	Published *Round-Up,* a collection of his stories.
1929	His one theatrical hit, *June Moon,* a collaboration with George Kaufman, opens on Broadway.
1930–33	His health seriously deteriorated, Lardner continued to work between and during

hospital stays. Publishes *Lose with a Smith* (1933) and a series of radio columns for *The New Yorker* from 1932–33.

1933   Died September 25 from a heart attack.

1934   Gilbert Seldes, at Scott Fitzgerald's recommendation, collected and edited *First and Last*.

1

The Only Quiet Man
in New York

The Niles, Michigan, *Daily Star* carried a lengthy
account of the wedding of Ellis Abbott and Ringgold Wilmer Lardner on June 28, 1911. One
paragraph enumerated some of the numerous and
very beautiful gifts, "among them being a solid
silver vegetable dish from 'Doc' White, the noted
Sox pitcher, who is a particular friend of the
groom; from the Cubs, a 200-piece Haviland set of
dishes; from Ben Johnson, Pres. of the American
League, a cut glass dish; Chicago *Tribune,* of
which the groom was formerly sporting editor,
electric lamp; from Jimmie Callahan, another
celebrated base ball man, set of glass-cut tumblers
and pitcher."[1] The elegance of these gifts sent by
Lardner's friends in baseball and newspaper work
reflects the esteem in which he was held. Furthermore, baseball players, newspaper reporters, and
wealth surrounded him much of his life.

To understand Ring Lardner, many sides of
his personality must be observed. He was, first of
all, inordinately kind. As a child he did favors for
people he liked, and he could not resist the appeal
of a friend in trouble. His earliest biographer,
Donald Elder, notes that from 1914 on, Lardner
gave away considerable amounts of money and
that during his most lucrative years in the 1920s,
he kept a virtual payroll of relatives and friends,

broken-down baseball players, or Niles boys in trouble; not even Ellis knew all of his secret charities.

Only his spending matched his generosity. In his early days while he was still in Chicago writing for the newspapers, he got a $5.00 raise. That sum boosted his weekly salary to $100; he spent $105. At his height, Lardner was making a handsome sum and spending all of it. Fears of early death compelled him to buy life insurance and at the end of his life, money was embarrassingly scarce. All that kept his widow in relative comfort was the life insurance.

By nature, and by his own admission, he was a prude. Even though much of his time was spent in pullman cars traveling with baseball players addicted to generally ungenteel behavior and in saloons and speakeasies talking to newspaper cronies, Lardner would not tolerate off-color stories. Sex is conspicuously absent (or at least intentionally underplayed) in his fiction and at the end of his career he waged battle through the pages of the *New Yorker* against suggestive lyrics in current songs. His son, Ring Lardner, Jr., judges that not only did Lardner's brothers and sisters share his basically puritanical attitude, "so to a large extent did the community they came from. Queen Victoria had no more loyal subjects, morally speaking, than in the proper households of the American Midwest. Episcopalians, Presbyterians, Methodists—whatever their differences, they shared the doctrine that sex outside the framework of marriage was an abomination. Ring's standards were just a more literal and rigid version of the prevailing view."[2]

A private man, Lardner destroyed most of his correspondence, dropping a letter into the wastepaper basket as soon as he had read it. He kept no copies of the stories he published. According to his son, he was "reserved, laconic, uneasy in crowds, with a mask over his emotions and a deep-seated mistrust of face values, a cynic who felt that if something could be faked, it probably was."[3]

He was a humorist who, if anyone asked, "Have you heard the one about . . . ?", left the room. Epithets describing him vary only in degree. Sherwood Anderson called him a solemn-faced man; Scott Fitzgerald referred to his habit of silence; John Berryman called him suspicious as W. C. Fields, silent as a Pharaoh; Hugh Fullerton described him at twenty-two as Rameses II, with his wrappings off. Others referred to his shyness and aristocratic aloofness, his laconic and saturnine nature, his elusive and enigmatic quality, his deadpan demeanor. He was, to still others, an oasis of silence, the only quiet man in New York.

The family into which Ring Lardner was born in 1885 was the epitome of society, wealth, and aristocracy in Niles, Michigan. His parents, Henry and Lena Phillips, Lardner came from established families, were practicing Episcopalians, and indulgent parents. Henry, third generation of a Philadelphia family, amassed quite a fortune and maintained his family in considerable affluence until 1901 when he, like many others, lost his wealth from overspeculation in land investments and excessive mortgages. Lena Phillips Lardner was a bright, vivacious woman, combining a

conventional and strict religious practice with an
unconventional social life. Guests and friends in
the Lardner household were invited because they
were interesting, not because they were socially
impressive.

The Lardners had six children—William,
Henry, Jr., and Lena (three others did not survive); twelve years intervened and they had three
more—Rex, Anna, and Ring. These last three
children were the indulged progeny of Lena's
middle age and they remained extremely close
throughout their lives. During childhood, the
house and grounds were their play world, the
family their closest companions. Provided with a
baseball diamond, a tennis court, a stable, and an
expansive lawn for winter sledding, these young
Lardners remained at home, never in the early
years venturing outside the grounds except in the
care of a servant.

This unusual upbringing in a small-town,
Midwest family kept the three young Lardners
somewhat isolated. Town children might be
invited to the Lardner house, but Rex, Anna, and
Ring did not go to other children's houses. With
the help of a tutor, Lena supervised their early
education until they all three entered the Niles
high school. They performed poorly on the entrance examination, but redeemed themselves and
completed the required work with ease.

Born with a deformed foot, Lardner underwent surgery in infancy and wore a metal brace
until he was eleven. The early care and attention
corrected the problem and almost no trace of the
lameness was evident by the time he was an adult.

Sports, particularly baseball, commanded the
out-of-door activities; inside, reading, musicales,

and dramatic spectacles entertained children and visitors alike. Lena, charming and witty, wrote plays, stories, and poems. Much of her poetry was published, but collections entitled *Sparks from the Yule Log* and *The Spray of Western Pine* show her verse to be in that popular and sentimental vein that decays with time. Her literary interest, however, spurred reading in the household and the children had to read everything without skipping. The Brontës and Dickens were among their favorites, but Ring Lardner remembered *Bleak House,* one of Dickens's longest novels, as being something of a trial for an eight-year-old to read with no skips.

An accomplished pianist, Lena saw to it that the family had musical training. Her daughter Lena was a fine organist and Ring was a frustrated musician all of his life. Musicales were performed at home; later Ring participated in more extravagant community productions at the Niles opera house. Dramatic readings must have provided much family entertainment, particularly with Rex and Anna reciting "The Raven" and with Ring, perched atop the bookcase, announcing "Nevermore" on cue. Lena often oversaw full productions of plays she had written for the children. Lardner's childhood was somewhat unorthodox, but he grew up in a lively, unconventional, and intelligent family—an excellent environment where his innate humor flourished.

By 1901 the family fortune had collapsed, but the household routine continued after a fashion. Financial matters were not immediately severe enough to force Ring to remain at a job longer than two weeks, the approximate time he lasted for three employers—McCormick Harvester;

Peabody, Houghteling Company; and the Michigan Central Railroad. A brief time at the Armour
Institute in Chicago failed to make Rex and Ring
into mechanical engineers, the profession their
father encouraged. After a time as a substitute
postman, Lardner settled down for a year and a
half, working for the Niles Gas Company.

Ring Lardner began his newspaper career by
accident (the editor had come to hire Rex) and
later in an autobiographical account, he listed his
early career in journalism. "Part of 1905, 1906
and part of 1907: Society reporter, court-house
man, dramatic critic and sporting editor for the
South Bend, Indiana, *Times*." His extensive
knowledge of baseball led the Chicago sports
writer, Hugh Fullerton, to recommend him to the
Chicago *Inter-Ocean* as a sports reporter.

The move to Chicago was important. On the
Inter-Ocean he got his first by-line and came to
know some of Chicago's leading journalists—
Fullerton, Hugh E. Keogh, and Charlie Dryden.
By 1908, Lardner had advanced to the Chicago
Examiner, writing a by-line under an established
pseudonym and traveling with the Chicago White
Sox on their spring tour. In the fall of 1908 he was
hired by the Chicago *Tribune,* and worked as a
sports reporter until December 1910. After brief
stints with *Sporting News* in St. Louis, the Boston
American, and the Chicago *Examiner,* he rejoined
the *Tribune* in 1913 and took over the well-es-
tablished column, "In the Wake of the News."
His name was known now to countless readers.
Using devices that Keogh had employed in the
column before him and developing other techniques of his own, Lardner delighted readers with
portraits of sports figures, poems, epigrams, letters
and verses (supposedly from readers or famous

baseball players), reports of his child's first hair cut, serials (like "The Pennant Pursuit"), very short stories, brief plays, and countless parodies.

Lardner's rapid and almost uninterrupted rise in newspaper work repeats the great American success story: by the time he was twenty-three, he was at the top of Chicago sports journalism. He achieved success because he was a meticulous writer and because he was skilled at finding and developing material. Producing a daily column of necessity brings forth inferior work, but the quality of so much of Lardner's newspaper work is excellent.

When Lardner resigned permanently from the *Tribune* staff in June 1919, he left Chicago for the East and on November 2, 1920, published his first "Weekly Letter" for John N. Wheeler's Bell Syndicate. This venture made him a national figure: one hundred and fifty newspapers with a total readership of eight million carried the "Weekly Letter." Topics ranged wide from the high price of coal to women's fashions. For the next seven years he continued the column amid extremely profitable financial returns.

From September 1922 to January 1925, he also did a comic strip based on *You Know Me Al* for the Bell Syndicate. This involvement provided no artistic satisfaction and Jonathan Yardley, Lardner's most recent biographer, argues that his agreeing to do the strip "is perhaps the most persuasive evidence available that he had also committed himself to a writing career in which financial gain would be the principal pursuit."[4]

Ring Lardner met Ellis Abbott of Goshen, Indiana, in 1906, courting her from the fall of 1907 until the summer of 1911 when they married. Their courtship was difficult since Ellis was finishing her last two years at Smith College and since Lardner was a sports reporter traveling either with the Chicago White Sox or the Chicago Cubs. Elaborate plans were necessary to effect meetings; train schedules and rainouts of baseball games often controlled their plans. Such prolonged separations made them dependent on letter writing which they carried on with great faithfulness. Hundreds of letters recorded their hopes, misunderstandings, daily activities, and occasional jealousies. Their courtship included a formal visit from Lardner to Ellis's father who had some reservations about his daughter marrying a man associated with baseball.

Their world in those years still retained some of the picturesque life of the late Victorian era, a world as Jonathan Yardley describes it, of picnics with strawberries and courtships at arm's length. It was the world before the war, a world not yet completely bewildered by the twentieth century.

They married and settled in Boston for a short time until they returned to Chicago. Here or in the suburb of Riverside they lived until 1919 when they moved East—first to Greenwich, Connecticut: then to Great Neck, Long Island; and finally to East Hampton, Long Island. Four sons— John Abbott, James Phillips, Ringgold Wilmer, Jr. (Bill), and David Ellis—made a lively and busy household. Family photographs show the boys as somewhat chuby youngsters. Their childhood activities and later careers show Lardner's distinct influence although he seems to have been a somewhat distant father, not surprising for a man naturally shy and laconic.

The children were supervised by a formidable nurse, Miss Feldman, but did not lack for pleasant undertakings. In *The Lardners, My Family Re-membered,* Ring, Jr., recalls that the main leisure-time activity in the family was reading books. All six would often be sitting on the living room floor, each with his book. Dickens and Jane Austen were among Ellis's favorites; Ring liked the Russians. The boys staged musicales inside and played various sports outside on a spacious lawn. (A professional football player was hired at one time to coach them.) All four attended Andover Academy but none of them finished college.

All four sons grew to be handsome men and all were writers. John was a sports columnist for *Newsweek* and the North American Newspaper Alliance, a World War II correspondent, and later a film and television critic for the *New Yorker.* Jim was associated with the *Herald Tribune,* and earned a by-line for his contract bridge column. Ring, Jr., wrote for the New York *Daily Mirror* before he went to Hollywood and film writing. In the early forties, David wrote for the *New Yorker,* often having three by-lines in a single issue. At one time, seven of Lena Phillips Lardner's eight grandsons were newspaper men.

Life in Long Island in the 1920s combined "the old rich who belonged to the Social Register and entertained in a decorous atmosphere of in-tellectual conversation and croquet-by-gaslight; . . . the new rich who did nothing but drink and play bridge and golf; . . . [and] people of talent who worked hard and made a lot of money but were not rich—theatrical people, writers and jour-nalists, composers and artists."[5] The Lardners were associated with the latter group. Their neigh-borhood included Ed Wynn, Eddie Cantor, W. C. Fields, Fanny Brice, and Groucho Marx. Of their many prominent friends, the closest ones were

Grantland and Kate Rice, and Zelda and Scott Fitzgerald.

The Lardners moved into their Great Neck home, The Mange, early in 1921; in September 1922, Zelda and Scott Fitzgerald came East and also moved to Great Neck, not far from The Mange. By this time, Lardner was already a celebrity, a well-to-do and established writer and older than Fitzgerald by eleven years. The two men were radically different and the friendship is somewhat remarkable. Lardner was constitutionally quiet, shy; Fitzgerald was flamboyant and vivacious, the golden boy of the Jazz Age in many people's eyes.

Life amid the affluent surroundings suited the extravagant tastes and ambitions of both men. Lardner desired to give his family every luxury after the lean years early in his marriage. Fitzgerald's spending power was, of course, legendary. Both men engaged in many all-night drinking sessions, Lardner growing quieter, Fitzgerald more volatile. During one session, Lardner corrected Fitzgerald's pronunciation of *The Egotist,* adding that he mispronounced many words. Any resulting irritation on Fitzgerald's part was brief.

Both were certainly affected by life on Long Island; in turn, their writing was also affected. Reporting a visit with the Fitzgeralds in Europe, Lardner wrote, "Mr. Fitzgerald is a novelist and Mrs. Fitzgerald a novelty. They left the United States last May because New Yorkers kept mistaking their Long Island home for a road house." Yardley suggests that "the perceptions of Great Neck that Scott and Ring exchanged undoubtedly played a large part in helping him arrive at the clinical disdain for opulent vulgarity that is so central to *The Great Gatsby*."[6] Lardner satirized this same excessive wealth, particularly in "The Love Nest" (1925), "A Day with Conrad Green" (1925), and "Reunion" (1925).

Fitzgerald and Lardner were genuinely interested in each other's work. Not only did Fitzgerald bring Lardner to the notice of Max Perkins, Fitzgerald's editor at Scribner's, he also suggested that Scribner's publish a uniform edition of his work. Throughout the years, he kept up with the sales of Lardner's books and frequently lamented that Lardner would not turn to a long work and a serious subject. He knew Lardner well in the early 1920s; Yardley and other critics agree that Abe North in *Tender Is the Night* is Fitzgerald's thinly disguised portrait of Ring Lardner.

Lardner's interest in Fitzgerald's work led him to read the proofs of *The Great Gatsy* with care, pointing out and correcting factual errors. He also expressed his uneasiness to Perkins when Fitzgerald toyed with possible titles for *The Great Gatsby*, favoring for a time *Trimalchio*. Perkins wrote Fitzgerald that when Lardner heard the title, he instantly balked and declared no one could pronounce it.

In addition to sharing mutual literary interest and friends, Fitzgerald and Lardner also fought with alcoholism. After a characteristic three-day drunk in 1933, Fitzgerald wrote to Perkins: "Am going on the water-wagon from the first of February to the first of April but don't tell Ernest [Hemingway] because he has long convinced himself that I am an incurable alcoholic due to the fact that we almost always meet on parties. I am

his alcoholic just like Ring is mine and do not
want to disillusion him, tho even *Post* stories must
be done in a state of sobriety."[7] There was, un-
fortunately, no illusion about the drinking problems of either man.

As a teenager, Lardner was over six feet and
bartenders in Niles, Michigan, did not question
his age. His drinking began innocently enough; liquor helped him overcome his natural shyness and
reticence. He maintained his composure and
talked clearly after his companions had passed out.
With distressing frequency, he went on the wagon,
but to little avail. He had become an alcoholic
whose periodic drinking bouts were legendary in
New York and Great Neck. In spite of sober
periods when he continued to write, the drinking
seriously undermined his health. Ring Lardner,
Jr., acknowledges that "marital discord is a
natural by-product of alcoholism, but my parents
somehow succeeded in avoiding all but the most
private manifestations of it . . . even close friends
of Ellis's outside the family have said they never
heard her speak of it. It was the overriding problem, insidious and insuperable, of their lives and
they both tried to pretend it didn't exist."[8]
Nevertheless, Lardner's production throughout his
life was considerable and while one need not
smooth over the problem of alcohol, one must re-
member that his work did go on in spite of it.

Although the account of who at the *Saturday
Evening Post* rejected Lardner's first story is
somewhat uncertain, "A Busher's Letters Home"
appeared in the March 7, 1914, issue and
launched Lardner's career as a fiction writer. He
wrote well over one hundred stories, several of

them in sequences. Almost all of Lardner's sequence stories were collected into volumes within two years of their original appearance. Three sequences revolve around the busher baseball pitcher, Jack Keefe—*You Know Me Al* (1916), Jack's baseball career; *Treat 'Em Rough* (1918); and *The Real Dope* (1919), the accounts of Jack's army experiences at home and abroad. All three volumes are epistolary, letters from Jack to his friend, Al Blanchard. Baseball provided a rich lode for Lardner; unfamiliar army life did not. In 1933, he collected six baseball stories about Danny Warner, but the result, *Lose with a Smile,* was thin and disappointing.

The "wise boob," Lardner's portrayal of the American middle-class character who bumbles and elbows his way through life, resisting grace and manners with singular skill, is epitomized in stories about Gullible, Fred Gross, and Tom Finch, collected respectively in *Gullible's Travels* (1917), *Own Your Own Home* (1919), and *The Big Town* (1921).

Gullible and Finch share some traits. Both see the folly of pretentiousness yet each in his own way wants to benefit from association with the wealthy. For example, Gullible will go back to the opera for no other reason than to see his name in the society page of the newspaper. Finch sees through the cheap facade of the wealthy, but gladly pockets his betting money won because he was privy to their race track tips. Gross, a Chicago police detective, is the least successful character of the three. His spate of tasteless practical jokes confirms his utter lack of finesse; his foray into suburbia brought problems and frustration, not the social acceptance he envisioned.

By the 1920s Lardner had taken his place as
a serious fiction writer as the reviews and sales of
three collections of his short stories clearly show.
Ring Lardner came to Max Perkins' attention
through F. Scott Fitzgerald who enthusiastically
promoted his neighbor from Great Neck to the
editor at Scribner's.[9] Perkins wrote to Lardner in
a tone of deference, saying he would not have
bothered him save for Fitzgerald's encouragement
and insistence. The result was a pleasant association and the appearance of Lardner titles from
Sribner's. *How To Write Short Stories* was
published in 1924 after considerable effort on
Perkins' part unearthed copies of the stories
needed. Since Lardner had saved no copies,
Perkins was forced to secure them from photographs of the respective magazines in the public library.

At Perkins's request, Lardner supplied a brief
and amusing preface, spoofing particularly the do-
it-yourself writing instruction books and remind-
ing the reader that "no school in operation up to
data . . . can make a great author out of a born
druggist." Self-mockery continued in brief para-
graph-introductions for each story and this tone
caused many reviewers to question Lardner's
seriousness. Important among the reviewers was
Emund Wilson who wondered if Lardner could go
on to his *Huckleberry Finn.*[10]

Following *How To Write Short Stories* were
The Love Nest and Other Stories (1926) and
Round Up (1929). With these publications,
Lardner's best fiction was now collected before a
wide reading audience. In September 1924, Max
Perkins wrote Fitzgerald that 12,000 of the 15,000
printed copies of *How To Write Short Stories* had

been sold. Fitzgerald expressed his view about Lardner's critical reception in a letter to Perkins. "The boob critics have taken him up and always take a poke at the 'intelligentsia' who patronize him. But the 'intelligentsia,' Seldes and Mencken, discovered him (after the people) while the boob critics let *The Big Town* and *Gullible's Travels* come out in dead silence."[11] Lardner had indeed "been taken up"; between the Literary Guild and Scribner's, *Round Up* had a splendid sale of over 100,000.

In 1925, Scribner's published *What of It?*, a potpourri containing articles Lardner had written while he was in Europe in 1924; "Bed-Time Stories"; four fairy-tale satires; "Obiter Dicta," pieces from the "Weekly Letter" for the Bell Syndicate and from magazine articles; and, for the first time in book form, his three most significant nonsense plays—"I Gaspiri," "Taxidea Americana," and "Clemo Uti—'The Water Lilies.'" This same year, Scribner's also reissued in a uniform edition, *You Know Me Al, Gullible's Travels,* and *The Big Town*. The reissues can be partly credited to Fitzgerald who in 1923 had outlined a uniform edition on the back of a menu at a lunch with Perkins. While the "menu-edition" did not appear as Fitzgerald listed the titles, the occasion showed how thoroughly he knew Lardner's work. His list included fairly obscure titles like "Symptoms of Being Thirty-Five" (1921) and "What I Ought To of Learnt in High School" which had appeared in the November 1923 issue of the *American Magazine*.

Between 1915 and 1927, Lardner published a considerable amount of nonfiction which reveals his continued versatility in subject matter and ap-

proach but does not add measurably to his literary
status. *Bib Ballads* (1915) appeared, a collection of
occasional verse (mainly about his children) much
of which had been in his column, "In the Wake of
the News." In 1917, Lardner published eight articles in *Colliers* under the title, "A Reporter's
Diary." Collected and published in 1919 as *My
Four Weeks in France,* the articles were strained
since Lardner was not at home as a war correspondent and never got close enough to the
battle lines to gather first-hand material. His work
here compares poorly with *Southwest Passage,
The Yanks in the Pacific* (1943), a fine book by his
war correspondent son, John.

The *Young Immigrunts* (1920) is a delight-
fully amusing account of the Lardners' move to
Greenwich, Connecticut. *Symptoms of Being
Thirty-Five* (1921), a somewhat nostalgic glance
at youth, also describes the symptoms that signal
middle age. When a man reaches thirty-five, he
"sets down after breakfast to read the paper. The
mail man comes and brings him 3 letters. One of
them looks like it was a gal's writing. He reads the
paper." *Say It with Oil* (1923), an answer to Nina
Wilcox Putnam's attack on husbands, settles the
score by attacking the foibles of wives. These three
pieces are brief and somewhat uneven. *The Young
Immigrunts,* by common consent is the best of the
three, amusing throughout while the other two
amuse sporadically.

Max Perkins suggested that Lardner write a
"sort of burlesque on those dictionaries of
biography" which were, to Perkins, "most astonishing pieces of bunk, written in all solem-
nity."[12] According to A. Scott Berg, Perkins discussed the biography burlesque at the same time

when he was urging Lardner toward a longer
work. The result was not long, however, and
turned into Lardner's purported autobiography,
The Story of a Wonder Man (1927). Not to be
taken too seriously, the work still entertains from
the preface by one Sarah E. Spooldripper (announcing the habits and the death of The Master)
through the sharp quips Lardner makes about his
famous neighbors in Great Neck.

Lardner's material appeared in various
magazines, particularly the *New Yorker* where he
published off and on from 1925 until his death.
Henry Seidel Canby accords Lardner a place of
considerable importance in the history of the *New
Yorker*. "The most influential magazine of the pe-
riod among sophisticated intellectuals, the *New
Yorker* (founded in 1925) had for its spiritual
ancestor the ironical, realistic humor of Ring
Lardner, with its notes of pity and its ruthless
satire of dangerous human types."[13] A few of his
verses and stories are there, but most of his
contributions were articles. Twenty-five came during 1932-1933 when Harold Ross made Lardner
the magazine's radio critic. The column, "Over
the Waves," was written under such titles as "An
Infant Industry," "Lyricists Strike Pay Dirt," and
"We're All Sisters under the Hide of Me."

By 1931 Lardner's health was so bad that
hospitalization was frequently necessary and
listening to the radio was all he could do. "Over
the Waves," a much-needed source of income, was
written from his hospital bed and bore headings
like "No Visitors, N.Y.," and "Do Not Disturb,
N.Y." In spite of illness and pressing financial
worries, Lardner still laced these columns with his
familiar puns, parodies, and witty one-liners. He

praised many singers and complained about others, especially Morton Downey, "God's greatest gift to the treble clef"; parodied phrases from popular songs and items from radio network gossip sheets; and particularly attacked the suggestive lines in song lyrics.

The puns are well illustrated in "The Master Minds," a contract bridge game supposedly played by John D. Rockefeller, Senator Reed Smoot, Miss Jane Addams, and J. P. Morgan. The latter shouts, "Haven't you read my book yet, Johnny?" The reply, "No but Oil read it in the Morgan." Fitzgerald referred to Lardner's "odd little crusade" against racy song lyrics; however, Lardner really thought such words had the power to corrupt. Titles like "As You Desire Me," "Forbidden Love," or "I'm Yours for Tonight" irked him considerably. Lardner vigorously resented any profitting financially from using indecency or sex appeal. Nothing made him madder, he quipped, except fruit salad.

As we shall see, the desire to write successful Broadway plays and musicals attracted Lardner's serious attention throughout his life. Although he had only one hit, *June Moon* (1930), he was for years associated in numerous ventures with prominent theatrical people like Flo Ziegfeld, George M. Cohan, and George Kaufman. His dramatic efforts in brief nonsense plays, however, have interested critics far more than his one Broadway sensation.

In sum, Lardner was a professional writer who spent much of his adult life meeting the deadlines of daily or weekly newspaper columns. Most of these articles remain uncollected. Many of his short stories have never been reprinted,[14] and of his collected stories, few have reached the contemporary reading public through anthologies. He was prolific, but he wrote to earn money. Although admired by some literary critics and by other writers, Lardner has nevertheless continued to be identified by this typical listing of his roles: newspaperman, columnist, humorist, writer.

Ring Lardner died September 25, 1933. The cause of death was a heart attack, but his physical condition had seriously deteriorated from tuberculosis, chronic insomnia, and alcoholism. When he died, he was forty-eight years old. On September 29, 1938, Scott Fitzgerald wrote a touching note of sympathy to Max Perkins who, Fitzgerald knew, had been so deeply hurt by the death of Thomas Wolfe. In doing so, he remembered Lardner's death five years earlier. "I feel like writing to you about Tom as to a relation of his, for I know how deeply his death must have touched you, how you were so entwined with his literary career and the affection you had for him . . . There is a great hush after him—perhaps even more than after the death of Ring who had been moribund so long."[15]

Three of Lardner's sons died early and tragic deaths. Jim was one of the last American volunteers to join the Spanish Loyalist army and one of the last to be killed in the Spanish Civil War. He was twenty-four when he died in 1938; his body was never recovered. In Hemingway-like words he had written to his mother his reasons for joining this army: "Because I want to know what it is like to be afraid of something and I want to see how other people react to danger."[16]

David went to Europe as a World War II correspondent. On October 9, 1944, he was killed when the jeep in which he, Walter Kerr, Russell

Hill, and a driver were riding hit a land mine.
David was twenty-five when he died.

In 1952, John was diagnosed as having advanced tuberculosis, but with new drugs available,
he made an extraordinary recovery. In 1957, he
developed multiple sclerosis and heart disease; he
died in 1960, six weeks short of his forty-eighth
birthday.

Fitzgerald, in 1925, wrote detailed instructions to Max Perkins about the arrangement,
jacket design, and advertising for his forthcoming
collection of short stories. The third item listed for
Perkins was a short line: "Dedication: To Ring
and Ellis Lardner." Now, in the light of the early
deaths of Lardner and three of his four sons, the
dedication of this particular title seems painfully
ironic. The book was *All the Sad Young Men*.

2

Common American

Ring Lardner's reticent nature not only made off-color stories distasteful to him, but also caused him to avoid what Hemingway espoused—the use of dirty words in fiction. While much of Lardner's life was spent in the company of baseball players whose social status was questionable and in saloons with newspaper friends, his private nature remained aloof from the unsavory side inherently associated with these activities. His purity of language was two-fold. Literally it was pure, *hell, damn,* and *sex* being about his closest flirtation with suggestive words.

The absence of "dirty" words drew Westbrook Pegler's praise, but in 1934 Hemingway found this very aspect a decided weakness in Lardner's writing. "Defense of Dirty Words" appeared in the September 1934 issue of *Esquire,* and here Hemingway played the devil's advocate to the supporters of the Legion of Decency and to all others hesitant about dirty words in fiction.[1] Hemingway charged Lardner particularly with having felt superior to that part of the human race he knew best. Such a stance, he declared, led Lardner to distort language when he wrote, especially when he wrote about boxing. "With never a dirty word [Lardner] wrote to these who make it with their hands in the nightly tragic somewhere of their combat, distorting the language that they speak into a very comic diction, so there's no tragedy ever, because there is no truth."[2]

As Carroll Grimes has noted, Hemingway's "Defense" brought sharp retorts from Alexander Wollcott, Heywood Broun who attacked Hemingway, and Franklin P. Adams who defended Lardner.

If Lardner was not a great writer, it was not his—to our notion—innate decency that kept him from being one any more than Mr. Hemingway's use in print of a lot of words that he uses many times a day, and most of the rest of us use with varying degrees of frequency, makes him a great writer. There was was [sic] no Nice Nellieism about Lardner, in or out of print; he hated meanness and pretentiousness with a scorn whose expression would not have been strengthened by the use of the dirty words that are in the vocabularies of most of us. For tough words do not a writer make, nor dirty stuff a page.[3]

The dirty word issue, of course, did not begin with Hemingway and of passing interest is a slightly earlier treatment of the subject. In the June 1923 issue of *Bookman,* Mary Austin published an article under the brave title, "Sex in American Literature," and took on the topic of dirty words.

Much of what is objectionable in recent fiction is of the sort that little boys chalk up on barn doors for other little boys to whisper and nudge about. It might get us forward a bit faster if there were fewer journals of literary comment so willing to become the barn doors of the current generation. But it is also indispensable to a growing society that there should always be little boys coming along able to be freshly struck with immemorial vulgarities and at the same time possessed of the normal instinct for getting them out of the system with a piece of chalk. The one really abnormal and unbearable person is the adult who prowls about looking for barn doors to froth over.[4]

Lardner apparently felt no compulsion to seek out
a barn door to chalk up and had he found one already chalked, he surely would have averted his
eyes.

Lardner's language was also pure in that he
caught the speech of his characters precisely. In
the *American Mercury* of July 1924, H. L.
Mencken wrote he doubted "that anyone who has
not given close and deliberate attention to the
American vulgate will ever realize how magnifi-
cently Lardner handles it."[5]

When Lardner reviewed J. V. A. Weaver's
In America for *Bookman* (March 1921), he gave
the author "a few pokes to the ear" and
demonstrated his own careful ear for speech.
Weaver had observed that people say *every-
thin'* and *anythin'*; Lardner disagreed. "We say
somethin' and *nothin'*, but we say *anything* and
everything . . . Mr. Weaver's ear has also give or
gave (not gi'n) him a bum hunch on *thing* itself. It
has told him to make it *thin'*. But it's a real effort
to drop the *g* of this little word and, as a rule, our
language is not looking for trouble." Further,
Lardner reminded Weaver that *feller, kinder,* and
sorter exist on the stage and in the comic strips,
but us common *fellas* say *kinda* and *sorta*. Lardner
regretted that Weaver's book had not mentioned
unquestionably the busiest adjective of that day—
lousy.

Lardner's style depends upon the almost
unerring language his characters use. Whether a
semi-literate baseball player or a talkative bride,
Lardner characters sound just as they should.
Their words are right and so is the rhythm of their
speech. Donald Elder has noted that Lardner
"was sparing of adjectives and wrote very little

description, yet even when he is writing in character, and usually an inarticulate character with a limited vocabulary, his language has an extraordinary power of evocation."[6]

A brief passage from "Women" (1925), shows how the language fits and identifies the character, Mike Healy, an eternal benchsitter on a baseball team.

"Oh, I've got a little money," said Healy. "I don't throw it away. I don't go payin' ten smackers a quart for liquid catnip. But they's more kinds of broke than money broke, a damn sight worse kinds, too. And when I say women has broke me, I mean they made a bum out of my life; they've wrecked my—what-do-you-call-it?"

"Your career," supplied Lefty.

Healy drops the *g* in *payin'*, his slang includes *smackers* for dollars and *liquid catnip* for liquor (prohibition liquor, that is), and he repeats *broke* three times, creating his own expression, *money broke*. His judgment is slightly awry—women "made a bum out of my life"; he should admit he has made a bum out of himself. He makes errors with subject and verb agreement—"they's more kinds" and "women has broke me"—and when he tries to recall the word *career,* he falters with "what-do-you-call-it?" while Lefty must give him the word. In spite of his considerable frustration over the supposed interference of his career, Mike's strongest word is *damn.* Obviously, his limitations as a baseball player are mirrored forth in what he says and how he says it. Excuses are his compensation for little talent and no success; his language gives him away before he even takes to the baseball field.

In "Ring Lardner: Reluctant Artist," Charles S. Holmes sees Lardner's greatest accomplishment in "the transformation of the speech of the American common man into a wonderfully expressive satiric medium . . . This is what Lardner did best—to create out of living speech a comic and distressing image of the American common man."[7]

When Ring Lardner took over "In the Wake of the News" at the Chicago *Tribune,* he began sharpening fictional and semi-fictional techniques that emerged as amusing parodies, burlesque, tall tales, short stories, and brief plays. The refining of his writing talent took time, but his planning was meticulous. Yardley describes him as an intense writer who rarely wrote a second draft. To be the mouthpiece for first-person characters "took extraordinary skill to be able to distinguish the subtleties of the way these people talked and thought, and then to turn them into effective fiction; it also required Ring's controlling intelligence to determine what went in and what stayed out, what was emphasized and what was underplayed."[8]

Mencken called Lardner's style common American and Howard W. Webb has described that style as the Lardner idiom, "a skillful blending of malapropisms, slang, confused pronoun and verb forms, mispronunciations, misspellings and rhetorical effects that describes socially and psychologically the characters who use it."[9] Lardner was most successful with this idiom when he wrote one-sided narrative forms—diaries, monologues, letters, first-person narratives, and nonsense plays where two-sided communication was undercut by non sequiturs. Essentially, the

Lardner idiom, Webb contends, creates and si-
multaneously satirizes a character. Content and
form, matter and manner complement each other.

Close examination of Lardner's writing
reveals various aspects that distinguish his style,
identify traits about his characters, and create a
good measure of humor. Most of his characters
cast themselves out of social respectability with
their verb errors. The hotels of Palm Beach and
the summer resorts of Long Island resist guests
who sprinkle their conversation with *I seen* and *I
done*. In addition to glaring verb errors, Lardner
also used *of* as an auxiliary verb; a typical Jack
Keefe sentence illustrates: "I would of threw him
out a block but I stubbed my toe in a rough place
and fell down." Several of his characters substitute
it for *ed* in past tense verbs as Danny Warner does
throughout *Lose with a Smile*: "They trade it him
to St. Louis."

Characters do not always express themselves
in the conventional manner. Jack Keefe refers to
disreputable people as the "riff and raff," but
Tom Finch uses the more common "riffraff." In
The Real Dope, Jack uses an idiom properly,
"Well Al jokeing a side," but later turns to his
own version, "Well Al jokeing to one side." Jack
is not the sole user of these expressions which appear in both forms in other pieces. Occasionally
this and that becomes *this in that*. In 1932 when
radio had become Lardner's single outlet, he de-
voted part of his June 4 *New Yorker* article to a
brief exercise in pronunciation for his readers.
They might see *Amos 'n Andy* in the listing of
radio programs, but, Lardner insisted, what
people said and heard was *Amos and Andy*.

Malapropisms crop up in many of the stories as well as in the parody, *Say It with Oil.* To defend husbands, Lardner asks, "Now what is the definition of a wife? Well, he [Webster] says she is the lawful consort of a man, and it don't require no Shylock Holmes to figure out that what he meant to say, but was scared to say, was, *awful* consort." Characters frequently mix formal words with slang producing humorous and incongruous diction. Speed Parker in "Horseshoes" (1914) stopped the first baseball "with his stomach and extricated the pill just in time to nail Barry at first base and retire the side. The next time he throwed his glove in front of his face in self-defense and the ball stuck in it."

Considerable humor comes from Lardner's imagery which frequently yokes outrageous and incongruous elements. When the pretentious Dr. Platt walked by the Finches (in *The Big Town*), Tom spoke and Platt "give me a look like what you would expect from a flounder that's been wronged." Oranges, the old husband in "The Golden Honeymoon" (1922), says, "is like a young man's whiskers; you enjoy them at first, but they get to be a pesky nuisance." A clothing image in "A Frame-Up" (1921) shows Lardner at his best. "He'd bought his collar in Akron and his coat sleeves died just south of his elbow. From his pants to his vest was a toll call." In *My Four Weeks in France,* Lardner describes the big crowd awaiting mail call. "We were all given numbers, as in a barber shop on a Saturday night." When the image extends throughout a long sentence, the satire becomes more complex as when Lardner takes on *Who's Who.* "Not since I got through the

Telephone Directory has they been a book that
give me so many thrills as Who's Who in America
for 1924–25 and have just finished reading same
and could hardly lay same down or hold it up
either on acct. of it weighing pretty near as much
as a grand opera chorus gal" (in *What of It?*).
The imagery finds its sources in familiar things—
flounders, whiskers, barber shops, opera chorus
women; but Lardner creates the comparisons
which are at once amusing and satirical.

Delmore Schwartz suggests that Lardner's
allusions belie the image of him as solely a sports
writer and make him instead a highbrow in hid-
ing.[10] Many of Lardner's readers who recognized
baseball names immediately (Chomiskey, Cicotte,
Johnson) may well have been nonplused to come
across the numerous literary and musical names:
Bernard Shaw, Henry Adams, Jane Austen,
Richard III of literary note; Rosa Ponselle,
Lawrence Tibbett, Brahms, Grieg, Beethoven,
Bach, the latest song hits from *The Bohemian
Girl,* and *Carmen* of musical note. Chapter six of
the spoof autobiography, *The Story of a Wonder
Man,* illustrates Lardner's delight and sophistica-
tion in using incongruous, and often anachronistic,
allusions. The language, for Lardner, is down right
racy.

Entitled, "How I Threw a Big Party for Jane
Austen," the chapter recounts the author's meeting Jane Austen "at a petting party in the White
House." M-G-M had lured Jane Austen to the
movie kingdom with an attractive offer to use
Pride and Prejudice as material for a seven-reel
comedy with Syd Chaplin in the title role. Placing
himself at the disposal of the little author, "or
Janey as we called her," Lardner entertains the

visitor until her departure for Hollywood. A high-
light of the activities in the East was a visit to
Albany, New York, to meet Governor Al
("Peaches") Smith, a great admirer of Miss
Austen's work. "I thought 'The Green Hat' was a
scream," he complimented her.

Exaggeration appears in myriad forms from
the ridiculous tales Jack Keefe believes to Lardner's endless tirade against Parisian taxis in *My
Four Weeks in France.* Not death from World
War I battles, Lardner declared, but "death from
a taxi is the most likely form and the most distressing, for under the Parisian law the person run
down and killed is the one at fault and the corpus
delicti is liable to life imprisonment or worse."

Lardner could spin out an involved com-
parison and amuse by substituting an unexpected
word; in this case, *bootlegger* appears when the
reader looks for *meal.* "Just like the League of
Nations failed to prevent war, so has prohibition
failed to even slow up drinking and not only that
but it has made same five or six times as expensive
so that nowadays the average family has quit eating all together and don't know where their next
bootlegger is coming from."

The supreme comic device for Lardner is the
one-liner which demonstrates his ability to be suc-
cinct and satirical. Many of them have the quality
of the aphorism—they are telling expressions,
pithy and brief, yet in Lardner funny and biting.
"Wives," he said in *Say It with Oil,* "is people
that thinks 2 ash trays should ought to be plenty
for a 12 rm. house." Another, "They |wives| are
people that think when the telephone rings it is
against the law not to answer it." In a quick line,
Lardner spoofed the niceties and absurdities of in-

troductions: "But do say if you feel like it,'Pleased
to meet you Mr. Harly. Got anything on the hip?'"

The epistolary technique, Wayne Booth
reminds us, declared dead many times over, has
been revived to excellent effect again and again.[11]
Since this technique allows the author to distance
himself from characters and action, it served
Lardner well, providing a mask for both authorial
involvement and for style. Edmund Wilson, recalling an evening he spent with Lardner and the
Fitzgeralds in April of 1924, recounts Lardner's
saying of himself, "I can't write a sentence like
'We were sitting in the Fitzgerald's house and the
fire was burning brightly.'"[12] Of course, he did
write straight English on many occasions, but the
semi-literate speech dozens of his characters used
was, apparently, easier for him. Examples from
three works—the "busher" letters of Jack Keefe,
Fred Gross's letters to brother Charley, and the
letters Danny Warner and Jessie Graham write
each other illustrate Lardner's particular skill and
his persistence in using the epistolary technique.

When Clarissa Harlowe appended a mid-
night postscript in a letter to Miss Howe—"This
moment the keys of everything are taken from me.
It was proposed to send me down: but my father
said he could not bear to look upon me"[13]—
Richardson achieved a sense of great immediacy.
This effective element is not prominent in the letters of Lardner's characters who write to tell the
events of ordinary days to ordinary people, to com-
plain, to justify their actions, to report their trivial
progress in the world. *What* these characters write
and *how* they write reveal them as utterly lacking
social graces, as harboring limited and petty
opinions about mankind, and as showing little

concern over inhumane behavior. If some lines emerge as withering satire, others are just plain funny.

Six 1914 stories, "A Busher's Letters Home," "The Busher Comes Back," "The Busher's Honeymoon," "A New Busher Breaks In," "The Busher's Kid," and "The Busher Beats It Hence"—collected as *You Know Me Al* (1916)—are the best examples of the letters Jack Keefe writes from various cities to Al Blanchard back home in Bedford, Indiana. He writes about his adventures concerning baseball and love in sentences ranging from 4 words (the self-revealing refrain, "You know me Al") to 182-word sentences. In the long sentences, *and* and *but* are the primary connectors. Stringing his thoughts together, Jack does not use words like *however, therefore, nevertheless,* or *consequently* that convey a sense of cause and effect or of time relation. Sentences are overladen with independent clauses and when subordinate clauses appear, they usually are short and simple—"how it came off"; "what I am going to do"; "that he knows I am suspended."

Misspellings are frequent and erratic as are errors in verb tenses and pronoun cases. Verbs most frequently used are pallid: *is, know, call, bet, read, ask, come, jump, throw, guess.* By far, Jack relies most on the verb *says* and can hardly relate a conversation in a letter without it. A telephone talk with Violet (prospective wife number 1) is reported to Al.

She *says* Don't you know me, Jack? This is Violet. Well, you could of knocked me down with a peace of bread. I *says* What do you want? She *says* Why I want to see you. I *says* Well you can't see me. She *says* Why

What's the matter, Jack? What have I did that you should be sore at me? I *says* I guess you know all right. You called me a busher. She *says* Why I didn't do nothing of the kind. I *says* Yes you did on that postcard. She *says* I didn't write you no postcard. [Italics mine]

At least in this passage, Jack sets off the parenthetical *well* and the nouns of direct address with commas; other matters like quotation marks escape him.

Jack describes people and things in un-imaginative ways on most occasions: the hotel "is a great big place and got good eats"; "Frisco is a live town"; veteran ball players are "old Birds"; women are "skirts"; Manager Callahan is "a funny guy." Sometimes his descriptions point to his naiveté as much as to his limited vocabulary. Having been to Chinatown, Jack writes, "Seen lots of swell dames but they was all painted up."

Double negatives crop up on almost every page; for example, "If Comiskey don't come back soon I won't have no more money left." Homonyms add to the overall humor as when Jack complains to Al about train sleepers. "I have road one night at a time but this was four straight nights. You know Al I am not built right for a sleeping car birth." When Jack uses an adage, it comes out slightly mangled. "She maybe ain't as pretty as Violet and Hazel but as they say beauty isn't only so deep" and he decided "it is too late to cry in sour milk."

Such a catalog of rhetorical infelicities is hardly unexpected from a semi-literate character and Lardner makes good use of them all. An additional aspect in Jack's letters, however, is especially noteworthy. Just as Jack spelled some names of cities correctly because hotel stationery was in

sight, some formal set phrases that he had heard
also appear. When they are juxtaposed to his ordinary English, the mixture is curious, halfway
out of character, and humorous. For example,
when Jack talks salary, he speaks of so many thou-
sand *per annum*. Baseball front-office language accounts for other words: "Come to find out, when
they [White Sox] sold me out here they kept a *op-
tion* on me and yesterday they *exercised* it." Other
passages are less easy to account for. "I told him
who I am and says "*I had an engagement to see
Comiskey.*" "*I made inquiries* round here and find
I can get board and room for eight dollars a
week." "*You have no doubt read* the good news in
the papers *before this reaches you.*" "Then I will
be glad to have you and the boys come up and
watch me *as you suggested in your last letter.*"
[Italics mine.] Like the fancy salutations and clos-
ings that adorned many an illiterate slave letter,
Jack's forays into these ultra correct phrases are
seemingly used indiscriminately. They sound right
and he uses them as he uses the double negative
because it sounds right.

Particularly appealing in Jack's writing style
are the folksy images he quotes or makes up.
Unaware that these figures of speech underscore
his weaknesses, Jack writes them to Al because
they come to him naturally. Kid Gleason, the
assistant Manager, chastizes Jack saying, "You
field your position like a wash woman." The
White Sox catcher consoles Jack who has been
sold to the San Francisco club with "very few men
no matter how much stuff they got can expect to
make good right off the reel." Scheduled to pitch
against the great Walter Johnson, Jack is warned
that getting runs off Johnson is "just as easy as

catching whales with a angleworm." A few glasses of Frisco steam beer and Jack feels "logey." Perhaps that condition accounts for his description of Hazel (prospective wife number 2) as "some queen, Al—a great big stropping girl that must weigh one hundred and sixty lbs."

The strain of black humor that many point to in Lardner's later fiction emerges in these earliest stories. Describing his pitching to Al, Jack uses an image that is familiar slang, but dreadful nonetheless. "Then I come back with two fast ones and Mister Pratt was a dead baby." A second example cannot be dismissed as slang and Jack's utter lack of perception is never more severely presented. Having made a fool of himself by giving his baby boy adult medicine, Jack reacts bitterly when his wife Florrie berates him:

If you want to kill him why don't you take a ax? Then Allen [Jack's brother-in-law, also a pitcher] butts in and says Why don't you take a ball and throw it at him? Then I got sore and I says Well if I did hit him with a ball I would kill him while if you was to throw that fast ball of yours at him and hit him in the head he would think the musketoes was biteing him and brush them off.

Throughout these letters to Al, Jack Keefe reveals himself to the reader as an egotistical and naive person who lacks sensitivity and common sense. His repartee quickly exposes his lack of intelligence. When Ty Cobb hit a line drive that was caught, he yelled to Jack on the pitcher's mound, "Pretty lucky Boy but I will get you next time. I come right back at him. I says, Yes you will." Jack is pleased with his smart reply which means the opposite of his intention. Equally revealing is

Jack's visit to the Boston wharf where he watches fish being unloaded. "They must of been a million of then but I didn't have time to count them."

For sheer humor, nothing in the letters surpasses the account of Jack's wedding expenses. The final item Jack entered in a list that included the fees for the license and the priest was "Tobacco both kinds $.25."

Jack Keefe, Lardner's most familiar character, exists through his letters. When he writes Al from abroad during the world baseball tour, from army training camp, and from World War I Europe, the predictably poor spelling and grammar errors appear, but the freshness and spontaneity of the early letters are not there. Heavy-handed reliance on spoofing, on practical jokes, and on the tall tale mars the seriousness that occasionally comes in. Both Jack and Lardner were uncomfortable abroad.

In 1915, Lardner published the Fred Gross stories in *Redbook*—"Own Your Own Home," "Welcome to Our City," "The Last Laugh," and "Uncivil War"—letters from Gross, a fat, beer-drinking Chicago police detective, to his Brother Charley. Although written just a year after the first Jack Keefe letters, these stories do not have the appeal of the busher's letters to Al. Lardner lacked the backdrop of baseball with its rich, familiar detail and characters. The Chicago Police Department, which might have served well, was apparently not an operation that interested Lardner. Gross is a police officer with a secure, if mediocre, position; but that office does not prevent him from "laying off from work," lying, and scheming crude practical jokes that bend the law considerably in their execution. Gross is as far from the ideal policeman as Jack Keefe is from the ideal athlete.

Policemen per se, however, are not the object of satire here but rather the "boob" who moves to the suburbs and makes ridiculous attempts to enter society. Satire is also directed at architects, construction companies, and real estate agents who control building, buying, and selling in the suburbs. Many of the headaches Fred Gross and his wife Grace suffer over building their suburban house find their source in the 1913 venture that Ring and Ellis Lardner undertook when they built outside Chicago in Riverside.

The epistolary technique reveals the aptness of Gross's name: his sentences are as improper and brash as his behavior is. In Jack Keefe's letters to Al, the reader is kept aware of Al as a silent character. Kind and generous, he assists Jack faithfully from leasing the little yellow house to loaning him money. Al, in other words, reads the letters and responds; Jack, in turn, acts on those responses. Brother Charley is frequently admonished to keep Gross's letters to himself, but the reader picks up no aspects of Charley's personality or habits. Like Jack, Fred Gross writes long, cumbersome sentences with main parts strung together with *and* and *but,* with distorted syntax, and with glaring errors in verbs and pronouns. His spelling is poor, but Lardner's use is sometimes farfetched—"& before Im threw with them they will be cralling on there hand and niece."

Fred's poor pronunciation of ordinary words marks his low social status: *ast, parler, im barrist, diffrunts, idear, morgidge.* A heavy use of numbers, fractions, and abbreviations indicates his ignorance of convention. Grace makes a visit "¼ of a hour" and Fred says, "Im the 1 that got the surprise." He uses the amersand, then the word *and*; other abbreviations include *Co.* (i.e., guests), *bet.*, (between), *wk.*, (week), and $ ("look like a million $"). Double negatives often emphasize the disparity between social expectations and Fred's attempts to fulfill them. "We haven't got no regular card party with prizes and refreshments." Malapropisms abound: the Hamilton's *higher* (hired) girl, the *vesty bull* (the vestibule), and firemen are to shut off the water *insolently* (instantly) are three examples among dozens.

Lardner constantly juxtaposes a social convention with Fred's absurd execution of it. Nowhere do Fred and Grace reveal their social ignorance more than in the invitation they had printed for a guest list of only five couples. Here Lardner's satire withers its victim.

F. A. Gross asst. Chief of Detectives Chicago Police dept. & lady will be please to entertain you Jan. 7 from 8 P.M. on. 3 tables progressive cinch followed by refreshmunts. Gents prize 1 qt. whiskey. Ladys prize hansome pare of corsets. Dress sutes.

The guests in "dress sutes" will be served "frank forters & liver worst & slaw & potato sellid & ice cream & cake & coffee & of corse beer." The Gross family in Allison sixteen miles from the Chicago loop, live in a comedy of errors, but Lardner strains too hard and in spite of effective humor and biting satire, the epistolary technique did not become a rapier for him here but a broadsword.

The letters between Danny Warner and Jessie Graham appeared in 1932, published in the

Saturday Evening Post as "One Hit, One Error, One Left," "When the Moon Comes over the Mountain," "Lose with a Smile," "Meet Me in St. Louis," "Holycaust," and "The Idea of June." Danny and Jessie are no more likeable than the Keefes and the Grosses, but they are at least sweet and dumb rather than arrogantly egotistical and dumb.

Here Lardner has two letter writers and the styles reveal each as timid, naive, inexperienced, and unpolished. Born losers, Danny and Jessie do well to "lose with a smile." In addition to the plethora of grammatical and syntactical errors, Lardner slips in a few devices that reflect the nonsense plays he wrote in the 1920s. Danny, of course is oblivious to the non sequitur when he writes Jessie that "mgr. Carey calls me Rudy like the rest of the boys is calling me and he is a good singer himself but can't groon like I tho when he was in school he studed for the priest hood."

Generally dismissed as a work of little success, *Lose with a Smile* does not stand up under close analysis. Nevertheless, the epistolary method does serve useful purposes. The Lardner canon includes "Some Like Them Cold" (1921), letters between Chas. F. Lewis and Mabelle Gillespie who ingratiate themselves until circumstances bring to light their true and unpleasant natures. Untalented and dull, Danny Warner and Jessie Graham are among the faceless nonentities of society. They lack brains, talent, imagination and at the end even the letters that should bring them together cross in the mail, leaving Jessie at Penn Station not really sure that Danny knows to meet her. But unlike Chas. F. Lewis and Mabelle,

Danny and Jessie do not dissimulate; they are what they are.

Nowhere in Lardner is the reality of empty lives better expressed than in these letters as one Jessie writes from her home in Centralia, Illinois, illustrates. "I am a poor hand at writing letters and there is so little news here, but the weather has been bad, rainy and snowing and it is hard to imajine you playing ball while we are having such nasty weather." The spelling errors have lessened, but the content offers little promise for the characters in life. They are all a sorry lot toward whom Lardner showed little sympathy and in whom his considerable pessimism is reflected.

Lardner frequently wrote in the first person, preferring that to the third by far, and published four first-person stories in the *Saturday Evening Post* between March 27, 1920, and May 14, 1921. Some critics consider the collected version of these stories, *The Big Town* (1921), the closest attempt Lardner ever made at a novel. In these stories, Tom Finch, the narrator who keeps the reader in his confidence, relates the adventures he undergoes with his wife Ella and her sister Kate in the Big Town (New York). Having inherited $75,000 apiece, the sisters find society dull in South Bend and head for the city to find Life and a husband for Kate. The lively first-person narrative gives Lardner leeway to have Tom Finch comment on the foolishness of the wealthy and the nouveau riche, describe people and their antics in folksy diction and colorful imagery, and survive the forays into the upper crust with eyes wide open.

A former cigar salesman, Finch helps his wife live off the interest of her inheritance but like the

maligned husbands of the comic strips, Tom is
never allowed to forget whose the money is. The
stories remain amusing because the reader sides
with Tom, sharing his cynicism and smiling at the
way he expresses it. Finch involves the reader by
saying, "But if you want to hear about it, I'll tell
you," and his humorous and sharp remarks show
him to be a man of little pretense. Unlike *Gullible's Travels* where the Missus is finally
humiliated in her futile attempt to hobnob with
with elite of Palm Beach, the trio in the Finch
stories are tougher, more resilient. The women
may shed a few tears, but not for long. After all,
their funds are considerable.

Through Finch, Lardner's satire ranges over
many targets to convey a sardonic view of men and
manners. Although willing to stop work, Finch
expresses disdain for the war profiteering that
made his late father-in-law rich. "His only regret
was that he just had one year to sell leather to his
country." The brief parody juxtaposes Nathan
Hale's true patriotism with Papa's situation—a
man who dies of grief because World War I ended
just as the profits for him were rolling in.

Finch's imagery and diction shatter all
pretense: Ella's and Kate's dignity wavers since in
the train diner they "talk like barbers." On the
first night in New York, Kate "had on the riskiest
dress she'd bought in Chicago." Dresses, Ella
insists, like the trip, are devices to get Kate a husband: there will be "quick returns on an investment." Once settled in New York, Kate meets a
series of men, each considered husband material, and Ella quickly champions their wealthy
neighbor in spite of his age. Kate, however, will

not encourage him and Tom bluntly reveals the man's dotage. "He'd seen baseball when second bounce was out. If he'd of started his career as a barber in Washington, he'd of tried to wish a face massage on Zackary Taylor."

Situated at a Long Island summer hotel, Ella and Kate continue the man hunt while Tom continues his sardonic observations. Exasperated by society women's banal chatter which moves ever so often to the comment, "The present situation can't keep up," Finch's comeback is "The hell it can't." When Tom introduced the English-woman, Lady Perkins, middle-class idiom solidifies his social status: "Then I done the honor. 'Lady Perkins,' I said, 'meet the wife and sister-in-law.'" Unimpressed by the wealthy, Finch describes the sparse activity at the hotel dance. Dr. Platt "had a gal with him that looked like she might be his mother with his kid sister's clothes on. Then they was a pair of young shimmy shakers that ought to of been give their bottle at six p.m. A corn wouldn't of bothered them the way they danced; their feet wasn't involved in the transactions." Not much about society impresses Finch.

Unsophisticated, Kate attracts dubious suitors and of the early contenders, her favorites are hardly social plums—a chauffeur and a jockey. The latter, Finch says, "was about Kate's height, and take away his Adam's apple and you could mail him to Duluth for six cents." Finch's opinion of the social gadding is never a mystery and is abundantly clear when he reports that "the two gals prettied themselves up every night for dinner in the hopes that somebody besides the head

waiters would look at them twice, but we at-
tracked almost as much attention as a dirty finger-
nail in the third grade."

Although an allusion to the Yahoo is directed
at Tom by Ella, the word is of Lardner's choos-
ing; however, the temptation to draw Swiftian
comparisons must be resisted. Unconvinced that
Lady Perkins is trying to start something with
Tom, Ella declares, "They's a catch in this seme-
wheres. You needn't to try and tell me that a
woman like Lady Perkins is trying to start a flirtation with a Yahoo. Let's hear what really come
off." Tom may have rough edges, but he is no
Yahoo in the true sense of the word. Lardner's
satire may at times be serious against Tom, but it
is in no way an exposure of the man as an utterly
despicable creature.

Lardner's style in these stories establishes
Finch and the ladies as middle-class people with
little social grace. Finch's speech is less crude than
that of Fred Gross; since Finch is speaking rather
than writing letters, few spelling errors appear on
the pages and the punctuation is usually correct.
Verb and pronoun errors, colloquialisms, slang
and folksy imagery abound because they identify
Tom, Ella, and Kate.

Throughout his career, Lardner found
parody a natural outlet for his satire and humor.
In June 1923, he prepared the seventh installment
of a *Bookman* series "in which various American
authors using well known tales, attempt to parody
themselves." Lardner's choice was Tennyson's
"Enoch Arden," rewritten in the style of *You
Know Me Al*. Although the piece is trite, Lardner
did get off a few good lines, as the set-up for the
pun on *washed them up* shows. "Well, Philip's

old man had a bbl. of money whereas Enoch's family was always flat and lived on fish. They never had to clean the fish because they said the waves had washed them up."

Late in his career, Lardner published "Odd's Bodkins" in the October 7, 1933, *New Yorker,* a parody of O. O. McIntyre (McIntyre's initials stood for Oscar Odd) whose column, "New York Day by Day," ran in some five hundred newspapers. Lardner laced the piece with eccentric juxtapositions of real people for a classic display of name-dropping. "Diary of a New Yorker. Home for a moment to slit my mail and found invitations from Mussolini, Joan Blondell, Joan Crawford, Joan of Arc, President Buchanan, Joe Walcott, and Louisa M. Alcott . . . Breaking bread in the evenings at the office of J. P. Morgan & Company and sat between Bernie Shaw, H. J. [sic] Wells, Charlie Dickens, Lizzie Barrett, Will Thackeray, Lottie Bronte, Paul Whiteman, and Bill Klem."

Say It with Oil, "Marriage Made Easy," "Love Letters Made Easy," the preface to *How To Write Short Stories,* and *The Young Immigrunts* are among the other parodies Lardner wrote. Frank Crane, a clergyman and the most widely syndicated of the American columnists at the height of his career, published essays which Amy Loveman characterized as "a composite of quotations, platitudes, truisms, glittering generalities, and a good deal of sound common sense."[14] When Crane brought out an essay on twenty rules for a happy marriage, Lardner followed with ten easy rules to replace Crane's tough ones. Reading Crane's rules, Lardner wrote, was enough to make a couple "say it can't be done and they decide to remain celebrates and then what is to become of them 2 grand American institutions, the home and rent for the same.''

By far the best of the lot is *The Young Immigrunts* which parodied *The Young Visitors* (1919), a work purportedly written by twelve-year-old Daisy Ashford and published with an introduction by Sir James Barrie. (Donald Elder says Barrie was widely suspected of having launched the highly amusing spoof himself.) *The Young Visitors* has long passed from public notice, but as Jonathan Yardley has pointed out, the humor in *The Young Immigrunts* is so successful that it can be read with no knowledge of the original.

In midsummer of 1919, Ring and Ellis Lardner moved from the midwest to Greenwich, Connecticut, taking their eldest son John in the ''lordly motor'' with them and dispatching the remaining three sons by train under the watchful eye of Miss Feldman. For the fictional version of this trip, Lardner changed sons so that Ring, Jr. was in the ''lordly motor'' and thus his namesake could serve as author. The details of the auto trip with its numerous stops and starts, mistaken routes, and flares of parental temper related from the child's point of view, make *The Young Immigrunts* one of Lardner's funniest pieces and best parodies.

Introducing his family, the youthful author writes, ''I may as well exclaim to the reader that John is 7 and Jimmie is 5 and I am 4 and David is almost nothing as yet you might say and tho I was named for my father they call me Bill thank God.'' When Father decides they would save time getting to Syracuse by driving through Lyons the way the railroad goes, Bill reports the reaction when that road came to an abrupt conclusion ''vs. the side of a stagnant freight train that was stone deef to honks. My father set there for nerly ½ a hour reciteing the 4 Horses of the Apoplex in a under tone but finley my mother mustard up her curage and said affectedly why dont we turn around and go back somewheres. I cant spell what my father replid." Nearing the end of their journey, Mother is left in Manhattan at the 125th Street train station to meet the rest of the family while Father and Bill go on to Greenwich to see that the house is ready. Bill reports this phase of the trip.

The lease said about my and my fathers trip from the Bureau of Manhattan to our new home the soonest mended. In some way ether I or he got balled up on the grand concorpse and next thing you know we was thretning to swoop down on Pittsfield.

Are you lost daddy I arsked tenderly.

Shut up he explained.

The brief nonsense plays Lardner wrote have elicited much critical notice. Few were actually produced, but the Forty-Niners did present "The Tridget of Greva" as part of a revue and "Dinner Bridge" was written for the Dutch Treat Show of 1927. Others cannot be performed because they have, in Gilbert Seldes's phrase, unexecutable stage directions. As Act I of "I Gaspiri" ends, one reads, "(*The curtain is lowered for seven days to denote the lapse of a week*)." "Taxidea Americana" includes a note that "*Acts II, III, and IV are left out through an oversight.*" "Cora, or Fun at a Spa" sets Act III in "*A Mixed Grill at a Spa. Two Milch Cows sit at a table in one corner, playing draughts. In another corner, is seated a gigantic Zebu.*"

These plays are set in unlikely, and often ab-
surd, places: the Fifty-ninth Street Bridge in New
York City, the interior of an ambulance, a one-
way street in Jeopardy, the Outskirts of a Parchesi
Board, The Lincoln Highway. Characters' names
range from conventional ones like Taylor, Chris-
tine, Joe, Cora to names of famous people as
members of the dramatis personae. "Abend Di
Anni Nouveau" lists among its characters Walter
Winchell, a nun; Heywood Broun, an usher at
Roxy's; Dorothy Thompson, a tackle; Theodore
Dreiser, a former Follies girl; H. L. Mencken, a
kleagle in the Moose. Odd names add to the
illogic. In "Cora," Bennett Plague's surname is
explained. "His mother named him Plague as a
tribute to her husband who died of it." "Clemo
Uti—'The Water Lilies'" includes Sethso and
Gethso, both twins, along with Wayshatten, a
shepherd's boy. Ridiculous occupations and iden-
tifications add to the nonsense. Desire Conly, a
Corn Vitter, and Basil Laffler, a Wham Salesman,
are in "The Tridget of Greva." Fred Rullman, an
acorn huckster is in "Taxidea Americana" while
Egso, a pencil guster, and Tono, a typical waste-
basket, appear in "I Gaspiri."
    Impossible family relationships are listed
which reach beyond the ridiculous to suggest, like
the dialogue, the absurd—the complete disruption
of harmony and order. "Clemo Uti" lists "Wama
Tammisch, her daughter" yet no mother's name
had been given, and "Kevela, their mother, af-
terwards their aunt" poses inscrutable geneology
problems. In "I Gaspiri," a husband and wife do
not share the same surname and the wife's given
name is masculine: "Ian Obri, a blotter salesman;
Johan Wasper, his wife." In the same play is
Ffena, their daughter, later their wife." "Taxidea

Americana" has family members sharing a surname but in confused relationships. "Thomas
Gregory, a poltroon; Mrs. Gregory, his mother,
afterward his wife."

The performances of "The Tridget of Greva"
and "Dinner Bridge" were received with great enthusiasm. Josephine Herbst has suggested that
such material published in the avant garde
magazines of the twenties sounds today like gib-
berish, yet "Lardner's half-dozen Nonsense plays
in *What of It?* are as good as ever. For in his
Nonsense writings, as elsewhere, he never lost his
sense of character, not even when he had his
people coming out of a bathroom faucet."[16]

That sense of character is essentially a trait in
human nature that Lardner observed as he
listened to hours of talk on pullman coaches, in
saloons, at lavish parties in Great Neck: people
talk, but do not listen; they have much to say, but
little they say connects with anything else. This
gloomy observation is central to the best moments
in the nonsense plays and while the ridiculousness
is funny, the tone is one of despair. The conversation in Act I of "I Gaspiri" takes place in a public
street in a bathroom where two strangers meet on
the bath mat and what they say is funny, absurd,
disconnected, sad.

First Stranger: Where was you born?

Second Stranger: Out of wedlock.

First Stranger: That's a mighty pretty country
around here.

Second Stranger: Are you married?

First Stranger: I don't know. There's a woman living
with me but I can't place her.

"Dinner Bridge," one of the longest nonsense plays, occurs on the Fifty-ninth Street Bridge. The chief engineer dropped his loaded cigar under the unfinished surface planking the day before the bridge was completed. Ever since, gangs of men have been ripping up sections of the bridge in search of the lost article. The play presents the workmen with their dinner pails, pausing while the meal is served by two formally attired waiters. All speak Crowninshield English except for lapses into native dialects. Of particular interest is the waiter who listens to the various anecdotes and then asks crucial questions such as, "Whom did she murder?" or "How long is she in for?" The moment he asks the question, he exits, puzzling the storyteller who asks, "What's the matter with *him*?" Taylor answers, "He's been that way for years—a born questioner but he hates answers."

The question with no answer, puns, non sequiturs, unlikely settings make the plays in one way an attack on sheer lunacy, as Gilbert Seldes has described them. Maxwell Geismar found their purpose simply entertainment and laughter achieved by removing objects, people, and words from their usual context, or from the logic and reason we expect as normal.[17] Edmund Wilson compared the plays to Dada. Donald Elder adds that "I Gaspiri" (The Upholsterers), first published in the Chicago *Literary Times,* was released in the *Transatlantic Review* in 1924 "with a note by the editor commending it to the attention of André Breton, a leading surrealist, hinting that Ring was doing what the Dadaists and the surrealists were trying to do, and doing it much better."[18] Others see these plays verging on the "nihilism often so unmistakable in Lardner's last years."[19] Jonathan Yardley calls them a dazzling collection of verbal and visual nonsense, wildly comic, antirational, "They stand firmly enough," Yardley proposes, "on their own unique merits; they do not need to be encumbered with the weight of any literary 'school,' for the only one they belong to is their own—Ring's."[20] The plays represent very few pages in the Lardner corpus, but at the same time they represent the full scope of his style which ranged from the semi-literate ranting of Jack Keefe to the highly sophisticated compression of "Dinner Bridge" and "I Gaspiri."

Generally Ring Lardner was most successful when he wrote in the first person and most humorous when the language was the ungrammatical vernacular of his cigar salesmen, baseball players, police detectives, unsuccessful song writers, or middle-class social aspirants. Too much time has been spent contemplating what he might have done if only he had used and developed his talent differently, as Fitzgerald and Perkins urged. A close look at Lardner's language and style, however, shows as much competence and variety as it does limitations.

In spite of his protest to Edmund Wilson, Lardner could write straight English in sentences, far surpassing his example of "We were sitting in the Fitzgeralds' house and the fire was burning brightly." *My Four Weeks in France* (1918), Ring Lardner's unsuccessful attempt to be a war correspondent, contains several passages of sensitive description which show a discerning eye and a sympathetic response to the ruptures and displacements war causes. From a sidewalk cafe, Lardner looked out on one moment of the war in France and described what he saw. In this instance, he

3

Harpies and Gold Diggers

Jonathan Yardley has suggested that Lardner "tended to divide women into two separate and absolutely hostile camps." On the one hand were "harpies, gold diggers, and two-timers typified by the women he had seen hanging around ballplayers; these were women who had somehow betrayed their sex because they were just as coarse as the men in their lives, and frequently more clever." Opposite these were women "who remained faithful to his pre-Jazz Age sense of femininity but who also had wit, humor, ebullience and style" and in this group were diverse women he admired—Zelda Fitzgerald, Kate Rice, Dorothy Parker, Claudette Colbert, his sister Anna, his wife Ellis, his mother Lena.[1]

Examples from the first camp exist in Lardner's fiction, but women characters seldom (and never in a fully developed sense) exhibit wit, humor, ebullience and style. The women he portrays vary in temperament, background, and ambition. Generally, they are either unpleasant or unwise, too aggressive or too subservient, too naive or too worldly-wise. Although most of the women characters are married, Lardner rarely shows a marital relationship that is happy, growing, and content. Instead, women characters struggle to survive, spend energy (and money) pursuing frivolous and senseless goals, and fail to act positively or to rebel successfully.

Lardner's extreme and acknowledged pru-
dishness accounts for the near absence of sexual
suggestions in his fiction. The absence of "real
ladies," however, is somewhat puzzling. His
mother was a remarkable and talented woman; his
wife was charming and intelligent. Certainly he
had sufficient models had he chosen to portray the
"lady" in fiction. Upper society may have been the
predominant milieu of both his boyhood and
adulthood, but his fiction, as Maxwell Geismar
has pointed out, was about "the development of
the American middle class in the 1920s whose special historian Ring Lardner became: that ignorant,
self-centered, materialistic 'high-polloi' [Lardner's
phrase] who rose to such quick success and power
on the easy money of the twenties, which followed
the slippery and often illegal profit of the First
World War."[2]

A clever and amusing view of women was *Say
It with Oil,* Lardner's 1922 answer to Nina
Wilcox Putnam's attack on husbands, *Say It with
Bricks.* Here humor overrides satire and wit
tempers Victorian views. The persona's grammar alone dispels any pretense or seriousness.
"Wives," the narrative voice says, "is people that
asks you what time the 12:55 train gets to New
York. 'At 1:37,' you tell them. 'How do you
know?' they ask." Nina Putnam had complained
that husbands were always late getting to the dinner table. Lardner's reply "to that is that when
the little woman says dinner is ready you can
generally always figure on anywheres from 10
minutes to a ½ hr. before they's anything at the
table but flies."

While Lardner's stories have many funny
episodes and quick lines as *Say It with Oil* does,

the humor usually arrives with a painful self-revelation, a display of naiveté, ignorance, or self-consciousness. The easy-going banter found in *Say It with Oil,* "Marriage Made Easy," and "Love Letters Made Easy" is missing. The fiction treats women and men seriously, pointing out their foibles, exposing their weaknesses, and satirizing their pretentiousness.

A frequent female type in Lardner's fiction is the insensitive, aggressive, harsh woman who centers her attention on material things and good times; domestic concerns are of no interest, children of little consequence. Such a character has always been an apt target for the satirist. For Lardner, such women reflected the newer times when maintaining a home for the pleasure and comfort of husband and children was not the ideal life to which all women aspired. In his fiction this character type remains especially unpleasant: she does not strike out for a challenging career, but simply maintains her role, neither feminine nor feminist.

In "Mr. and Mrs. Fix-It" (1925), the two husbands play active and almost interchangeable roles with their wives. Furthermore, the victims (Ada and her husband, the narrator) are satirized as soundly as are the aggressors (Belle and Tom Stevens). Of all the meddlesome friends Ada has forced on her husband, the worst is the Stevens couple whom Lardner portrays as the busiest of busybodies. A total stranger, Belle overhears Ada ask a trainman directions, supplies them herself, and pounces into Ada's life. Quickly the narrator renames the Stevenses Mr. and Mrs. Fix-It as the new friends insist Ada and her husband break their lease and move to Chicago's North side, preferably into the Stevens's apartment building. Belle declares that Ada does not know how to buy proper clothes, hire a new cook, or get a suitable haircut. Tom informs the narrator that he should use a regular razor, buy different cigarettes, get better liquor, and be shrewder in buying a car. In desperation, Ada and her husband keep their long-awaited trip to Miami a secret, only to have Belle and Tom find out and fix things by changing the train line, the berths, the hotel, and the vacation clothes as well as by issuing instructions on how to vacation in Miami. Ada and her husband go instead to Biloxi—hardly a traveler's paradise— once Belle and Tom announced they planned to come along to Miami.

While it is easy to find the behavior of the Stevens couple maddeningly officious as they insensitively disregard the other couple's tastes, preferences, and plans, Ada and her husband are not faultless. When Lardner has the narrator describe Ada as "one of these kinds of people that just can't say no. Which is maybe why I and her is married," he portrays ineffectual characters ill-equipped to deal with problems. Indeed, issuing insults is the only recourse the narrator has against Stevens "and nothin' we could say was an insult." Furious complaints about Stevens do not stop the narrator from asking him to fix a speeding ticket—"it's silly to not appreciate favors like that." As much as Ada wants to keep the Miami trip a secret, she blurts out the news rather than have Belle and Tom think them too poor to join a California excursion the Stevenses proposed. In short, Lardner exposes all four: Belle and Tom are not malicious, but they are meddlesome and insensitive; Ada and her husband resent being pushed around, but will profit when the occasion suits and will protect their pride at all costs.

While "Liberty Hall" (1928) also deals with the busybody, Lardner sets the story in the East and Mrs. Thayer easily surpasses Belle Stevens in brashness. Ben Drake, a successful song writer and rival of Gershwin, has his privacy protected by his wife (who declines social invitations because they interfere with his work) and by his secretary (who sends a bogus telegram on his rare visits in case he needs an escape). Previous visits have been marred because Drake's demands were not all met: the bathtub filled too slowly, the breakfast was skimpy, the reporters still reached him, no bedside lamp was provided. "Liberty Hall" recounts the visit that ended visits for Drake.

The peaceful week's stay arranged for the Drakes (the Thayers' house will be "Liberty Hall") turns into a cabal with Mrs. Thayer at every turn ordering activities Ben Drake detests and forbidding those he enjoys. The final straw comes when Mrs. Thayer intercepts the bogus telegram, memorizes its contents and then disposes of it after answering it herself to keep Drake's visit uninterrupted. In desperation, Drake claims a premonition, tricks her into divulging the telegram, and promptly leaves to answer its summons.

Lardner's satire remains relatively mild here, but his treatment of the four characters is critical nonetheless. Mrs. Thayer displays no feminine charm; instead, she pushes, manages, and arranges. Her husband is given little to do or say, powerless against her domineering ways. Ben Drake takes his wife for granted, leaving her to endure solitary days and nights when his play is in rehearsal. Lonely, she needs the invitations he refuses. The social rank of the respective couples in "Mr. and Mrs. Fix-It" and "Liberty Hall" shifts from a modest Chicago flat to the Thayers' estate, Landsdowne; instead of the elevated train, characters travel in a limousine; the narrator can only insult Tom Stevens, but Ben Drake goes on a binge after escaping from the Thayers. His wife shows little surprise when she says, "small wonder that Ben was credited at the Lamb's Club with that month's most interesting bender." Higher social position with affluent surroundings does not improve people and while Lardner makes us laugh, we are laughing at undesirable traits.

Not only is the nurse Miss Lyons in "Zone of Quiet" (1925) an insensitive woman, she also lacks all of the expected qualities of her profession. As the doctor leaves the patient who is not fully awake from anesthesia, he tells Miss Lyons not to let the man talk "and don't talk to him; that is, if you can help it." Once the doctor is out of ear shot, Miss Lyons begins with a ceaseless chatter. Self-centered, she relates that her friend Marian's boyfriend is second-rate, yet admits stealing him and quickly demeans him in her account of Marian's winning him back. Thoughtless, she weaves in facts about her recent patients, all of whom have died. Unprofessional, she comes on duty late and sleepy from having danced until early morning, chews gum because she is nervous from lack of sleep, and makes light of her state board examinations. It is ridiculous, she says, to be asked "Is ice a disinfectant?" because ice not used in highballs is wasted. After several days of so much talk, the patient has been kept from his book, *Vanity Fair,* with whose scheming heroine Miss Lyons shares several traits.

To dismiss the nurse as a mere featherbrain, as some have done, is to judge the story too lightly. Miss Lyons's youth and good looks do not compensate for her inept and somewhat sadistic behavior. She does not give the patient time to say that he slept poorly and she stands far removed from the ideal nurse who is kind, efficient, prompt, alert, and sensitive. Just as Jack Keefe in *You Know Me Al* flagrantly disregarded baseball training rules and managerial orders, so Miss Lyons has no sense of duty, no concern for her patient's well-being.

Women play an important role in the life of Jack Keefe, Lardner's baseball player-boob who became a familiar figure when "A Busher's Letters Home" appeared in the *Saturday Evening Post* in 1914. Writing to his hometown friend Al Blanchard, Jack relates his ups and downs as a baseball player, as a husband, and later as a none-too-willing soldier. His common theme is steadfast: whatever has gone wrong is no fault of his. The letters quickly reveal his naiveté, his willfulness to break rules, and his irresponsibility. With such undesirable traits, he is at best a dubious judge of others. A disingenuous narrator, Jack reports and the reader evaluates. What Jack says about marriage and his wife Florrie is colored with snide and bitter remarks. Whether or not Florrie deserved the sorry opinion Jack held about her is debatable; however, what he tells and how he tells it strongly suggest that Florrie used him, spent his money, and ignored his difficulties.

Marriage to Florrie has not made Jack happy or content. When his baseball team stopped over in Salt Lake City, Jack wrote to Al that this place must be populated with boobs "because they tell me some of them has got ½ a dozen wives or so. And what a man wants with 1 wife is a mistery to me let alone a ½ dozen." Life with Florrie proves to be a dismal experience. Anxious to be in Bedford with Al and his wife Bertha, Jack rents the little yellow house. (In the first six busher stories, Jack frequently apostrophizes, "O, little yellow house," the line running as a refrain recalling the past, and hinting of illusive happiness.) Florrie, however, has no interest in meeting the Blanchards, much less in living even part of the year in a small Indiana town. When a short delay alters the latest departure to Bedford, Florrie announces that a six-year wait would suit her.

Jealous of the time Jack spends writing to Al, Florrie's attitude toward the Bedford friends grows callous and rude. She suggested that Bertha should probably just stay home rather than visit the Keefes in Chicago; sent them word at Christmas that "we are well supplied with pin cushions now because the one you sent makes a even half dozen"; and told Jack that she would use the baby dress Bertha made for Jack and Florrie's baby as a dishrag. Although Jack adds in his letter, "I guess she didn't mean it," the reader knows she probably does.

Careless with money, Florrie leads Jack into buying clothes and furniture they do not need and into supporting her sister and brother-in-law. Her reaction to Jack's failures to get advances and raises is to berate him, then to cry and rue the day she married him. Florrie is not domestic: a hired girl cleans the flat (usually with four adults underfoot) and another girl looks after little Al so that Florrie can operate a beauty shop. Soon her income surpasses Jack's and since she can support herself and the child, Jack's army deferment is dropped and off he goes to Camp Grant, Illinois. Florrie rarely visits Jack even though the camp is nearby and when she does finally come, her lack of concern is epitomized both in what she brought and in what she did not bring.

But I didn't feel so sorry for him [a fellow soldier] when we opened up the boxes they had broughten us and Sebastian's wife had give him doughnuts and a pie and part of a cake and goodys of all kinds and when I opened up my box it was a lb. of candy like you get in union station for 60 ct and if it wasn't for the picture of a girl on the cover it would be all profit and a man can't eat the picture which was the only part of it that hadn't ran together like chop sooy and Florrie would of made just as big a hit with me if she had of put in the time baking me a mess of cookys that she spent toneing up her ear lobs or something.

Jack's army life makes him increasingly bitter when he speculates about death. If he has meant so little to Florrie alive, dead he will be worth hardly a thought. "I suppose if I die where she can tend the funeral she will come in pink tights or something." In another letter, Jack tells Al that if Secretary of the Navy Daniels wired Florrie and little Al "that Jack Keefe had been killed they would say who and the hell is he."

Jack probably did not deserve any better treatment than he got, but Florrie only wants to spend more money, go more places, and have more things. As long as Jack can meet her demands, their life goes along rather well; however, when funds get low and debts mount, harmony disappears. Jonathan Yardley described Florrie as "a gold-digging shrew": Donald Elder called Jack's marriage one of constant bickering. Abrasive and

unfeminine, Florrie is one of Lardner's most unpleasant women characters, quite the opposite of
the ideal woman he saw in his mother and his
wife.

In contrast, many of the women characters
are (or seem to be) patient, quiet, and faithful.
Ironically, the best example of this type never appears, but is merely referred to. Bertha Blanchard,
Al's wife, supports her husband's willingness to
remain Jack Keefe's friend, loaning him money,
arranging house rental, accepting the various
responsibilities Jack casts upon him. The reader
pictures Bertha as implicitly a good woman,
possessing all the domestic interests and virtues
Florrie lacks.

Representative of the patient woman is
Mabelle Gillespie, that quiet, thrifty, efficient girl
in "Some Like Them Cold" (1921), who in reality
just connives to get a man. Radically different are
Julie Gregg ("Haircut," 1925) as well as Ellen
Kelly and Emma Hersch Kelly ("Champion,"
1916), who are victimized by wicked men. The
Missus in "Gullible's Travels" (1916) is socially
ambitious, but when her Palm Beach fiasco is
done, she quietly admits her failure and returns to
her dependable domestic scene. Celia Gregg ("The
Love Nest," 1925) marries false expectations and
confronts her misery with heavy drinking and
silent protests. Finally, Bess Taylor in "Anniversary" (1928) pays a bitter price for being the
respectable wife in a respectable and model marriage.

"Some Like Them Cold" (adapted in 1929 as
June Moon, Lardner's one successful theatrical
venture) presents Mabelle Gillespie, a young
woman working in Chicago who by chance meets

Chas. F. Lewis in the Lasalle Street railroad station. Mabelle is waiting for her sister; Lewis is
waiting for the New York train, bound he thinks
for fame and fortune as a Broadway song writer.
An epistolary courtship of sorts ensues.

Portraying herself as thrifty, hard-working,
and domestic, Mabelle catalogs her virtues and
casts herself as a woman dedicated to making a
husband happy. The truth, however, is that
Mabelle merely wants to get a man and lures
Lewis with her amusing conversation, expert
housekeeping, and enviable cooking. Lewis's letters are full of poor grammar, misspellings,
clichés, and confused words, but Mabelle flatter-
ingly calls him a genius. Although Lewis had said
he did not want a wife "that don't know a dishrag
from a waffle iron," he does not propose to the
hopeful Mabelle, but instead marries his librett-
ist's sister. His wife will not, at least, confuse
dishrags and waffle irons since "she don't hang
around the house much as she is always takeing
trips to shows or somewheres."

Mabelle accepts her defeat with little grace
and writes Lewis a final letter which ends with a
sarcastic dig at his salary. "I am sure she is to be
congratulated too, though if I met the lady I would
be tempted to ask her to tell me her secret, namely
how she is going to 'run wild' on $60." Mabelle
and Lewis are typical of Lardner's middle-class
characters who lack charm and manners and who
are destined for mediocrity.

Unlike Mabelle, women in two of Lardner's
most celebrated stories, "Haircut" and "Champion," are ill-treated by men—physically abused,
neglected, humiliated. Jim Kendall and Midge
Kelly lack all vestige of humane conduct and dis-

tort the roles of the husband and son as provider and protector. The women are rendered powerless and the surrounding characters (the town population in "Haircut" and the prize fighter's public in "Champion"), while innocent of violent deeds, are still culpable because they do not act against these men.

Jim Kendall played appalling practical jokes, but when the innocent Julie Gregg became his victim, the result was Kendall's death. Narrated by the town barber as he gives a haircut, the story remains one of Lardner's bitterest condemnations of small town meanness. Never missing a snip, the barber relates Kendall's shabby treatment of his wife. Irked that she tried to garnishee his wages before he consumed them in gin, Kendall retaliates by having his wife and two children show up at the circus to meet him and get tickets he never intended to buy. His cruelty grows increasingly sadistic, but even in retrospect, the unperceptive barber laments Kendall's death declaring, "He certainly was a card."

His victims are vulnerable and innocent. Unable to force his attention on Julie Gregg, Kendall tricks her into coming to Dr. Stair's office at night. There, she discovers not the young man of her affections, but a small mob of ruffians who hound her all the way home jeering. Paul Dickson, a slow-witted fellow befriended by Stair and Julie, hears of her distress, goes on a duck hunting trip with Kendall (who had planned to push Paul in the water as a joke) and kills him.

Probably Lardner's most anthologized story, "Haircut" portrays Kendall's wife as helpless in her dilemma: life with Kendall is unspeakable but divorce is impossible because she has no means of support. The humiliation scene for Julie is all the more frightening because it occurs at night, Kendall and the pool room crowd are drunk, and Julie expected Ralph Stair to greet her so convincing had Kendall's voice imitation been. Critical commentary on the story has praised Lardner's excellent use of the disingenuous narrator and his thorough condemnation of a small town that tolerates a Jim Kendall. The women characters should also be carefully considered for in their helplessness against sheer brutality, they confirm that society can tolerate astonishing behavior without serious protest.

A catalog of Midge Kelly's exploits in "Champion" sounds like exaggerated melodrama, but like the adventures in *Candide* where the rapid cumulative effect creates the sense of unreality, no one doubts the truth of the individual deed. Kelly beats up his younger crippled brother for a fifty-cent piece, hits his mother, and gets out of town with money he forced from a friend. With success in the prize fighting ring behind him, he brags that he can kill his opponents, throws a fight for $80, and refuses to pay up his bar bills. Forced to marry Emma Hersch, he leaves her on the wedding night with a crushing blow on her pale cheek. He fires the manager who had pulled him from the gutter to riches, hires a new one, and promptly steals his wife. Money, fame, women surround him in New York. Yet short, pathetic letters from Emma and from Ellen asking relief from acute financial distress go unanswered while the current girl friend squanders $500 in a week.

A vulgar egotist, Kelly exemplifies the worst that wealth can produce. Lavish with money for new clothes, Midge selects with the taste of a

hayseed circus barker given an unexpected bonus.
"His diamond horse-shoe tie pin, his purple cross-
striped shirt, his orange shoes and his light blue
suit fairly screamed for attention." His senseless
extravagance makes the disregard of his family's
need all the more offensive. Like Jim Kendall,
Kelly is an amoral creature, vicious to women or
anyone else who gets in his way.

Lardner salvages the story from complete
melodrama by keeping Midge's road to success
unbroken and by never giving him the slightest
regret for his behavior. Instant pleasure fills his
mind; no suffering touches him. Singular in his
callousness, Midge will not protect, support, or
love the women dependent on him. Wife and
mother and child are left destitute and helpless.

"Gullible's Travels," Lardner's classic story
about the hazards of trying to overstep one's social
boundary, is narrated by the husband. The plot
begins when the narrator and his wife fancy
themselves above the "riff and raff" who enjoy
rummy games, "pitcher shows," and dancing at
Ben's and set out to "get acquainted with some
congenial people . . . people that's tastes is the
same as ourn." Their expensive attempt to hobnob
with the "E-light" in Palm Beach ends in dismal
failure when the Missus, unable to meet anybody
of consequence, is mistaken by *the* Mrs. Potter
of Chicago for the hotel chambermaid and
admonished to get towels for Room 559.

Although the husband agreed to sell stock to
finance the trip, his version of the events lets all
the humiliation fall on the wife. At the outset, he
gossiped with her over the adventures of the
wealthy recorded in the society pages of the newspapers. "We kidded and kidded till finally, one

night, she forgot we was just kiddin'." The longing to associate with the rich displaces logic and
common sense. In a final desperate attempt to
strike an acquaintance, the Missus steps on a
lady's white shoes in order to apologize. Her social
ineptness is painfully clear when she says to
another lady, "we got the coolest room in the
hotel, and I'd be glad to have you go up there and
quit perspirin'." The wife spends as much time
crying over failures as she does facing the im-
pregnable social frontier and must, in the end,
admit she has learned her lesson.

Laconic and cynical about prices, tips, and
hotel liquor arrangements, the husband remains
above any real concern over things but admits the
trip resulted from "I and the wife being hit by the
society bacillus." Never in doubt about the out-
come, the reader watches to see how thorough the
humiliation will be. The couple's inevitable failure
is hinted at by the husband's descriptions. "We
didn't have to ask the waiter if they'd [gluttonous
table companions] been there. He was perspirin'
like an evangelist." Their faulty grammar and
their naiveté spell certain doom in society:
"Here," I says, "they've give us the wrong room."
Then my wife seen it and begin to squeal.
"Goody!" she says, "We've got a bath! We've got
a bath!"

Perhaps new money may edge its way into
Palm Beach society, but a two-week budgeted vacation is nothing more than a wasted attempt.
Lardner frequently takes his characters out of the
social milieu they are accustomed to. When they
change stations, their happiness is measured by
their funds, and even in *The Big Town* where
money is plentiful for the Finches, happiness

comes in getting back home. In the end of "Gullible's Travels," the Missus sighs with some contentment, "Ain't it grand to be home!"

The vulgarity and menace of wealth are clearly shown in "The Love Nest" where motion picture producer Lou Gregg has successfully transformed his talented starlet wife into drunken chattel without ever letting the public suspect the slightest flaw in his happy home. Described as the great man, Gregg's garage shelters a Rolls, a Pierce, and a glittering chauffeur; his house boasts an *arc de triomphe* gate, Urbanesque landscaping, and a living room "that was five laps to the mile and suggestive of an Atlantic City auction sale." Considered a great home girl, Celia goes through the motions Lou demands: constantly greeting him with "Sweetheart," she strikes the pose of a woman for whom "home and kiddies come first."

On the surface, nothing about the plot is unusual: big money can buy everything, even the appearance of happiness. What distinguishes the story is the extent of Celia's despair, made bearable only through liquor. To Barlett, the magazine interviewer, Celia confesses her state. Since Gregg is often away and does not seriously question Celia's evening headaches, her late risings, or the half-filled bourbon bottles, he thinks that his money has bought him a happy wife and family. The pathos of Celia's life is revealed in the game she plays to keep Lou Gregg content. Further, allusions to famous theatrical greats—Francois Delsarte, Ina Claire, Ethel Barrymore, and Anna Pavlova—suggest Celia's efforts to keep alive remnants of the career she has lost. When Barlett arrived, she "made an entrance so Delsarte as to be almost painful" and greeted the guest "in a voice reminiscent of Miss Claire's imitation of Miss Barrymore." When she danced alone to the radio's music, she impressed Barlett with her skill but she protests, "I'm no Pavlowa." [sic] At twenty-seven, she is imprisoned in elegance, surrounded by wealth, children, and a husband she loathes.

Not entirely blameless ("I married him to get myself a chance"), Celia can only rue her life. Should she live long enough to witness her daughters grow up, she will advise Norma, who resembles her, "to run away from home and live her own life. And *be* somebody! Not a *thing* like I am!" Contemplation of divorce amounts to nothing: Gregg has done nothing indiscreet, and men avoid Celia because they fear him. Not a slick story about the idle rich, "The Love Nest" is a vicious picture of success. Gregg has built the image he wants the world to believe and Celia must play her part, relieved only by the senselessness that liquor brings. Denigrated, she is a *thing* and as much a victim of her fate as Midge Kelly's battered wife.

Death by boredom is what Bess Taylor faces in "Anniversary" as her husband Louis proves year after year how solid, respectable, and thrifty he is. When she married nine years ago, Bess was one of the town's "most charming and beautiful women"; now at thirty-three, her evening activities consist of forty games of solitaire (with occasional cheating) before bedtime. Louis will not learn to play bridge, the picture show hurts his eyes, and he will not allow Bess to go out alone at night.

To entertain Bess, Louis repeats events from his dull life and reads aloud from the Milton *Daily*

Star and the Milton *Weekly Democrat.* His selections are the fillers newspapers poke in to adjust
spaces and he entones such mindless trivia as,
"Although Edinburgh, Scotland, had only 237
icecream parlors last season, the number was fifty
more than were in the city a year ago."

The bitter irony emerges when Florence
Hammond appears to report a flat tire. While
Louis helps with the repair, Florence minutely
details the life of her sister Grace whose husband
buys her presents, goes on binges, and occasionally
hits her. Predictably, Florence concluded that Bess
and she can consider themselves lucky in having
solid, respectable husbands. But to Bess, violent
abuse surpasses boredom and neglect. Lardner indicates that Bess's dilemma is not to be taken
lightly. Louis keeps her in a comfortable condition, utterly oblivious to her as a woman or as a
person. She is Celia Gregg in small-town, middle-
class surroundings enduring life with solitaire
instead of bourbon. Her bleak prospects are
evident when Louis, defending his thriftiness,
explains about rainy days and old age. Her death
wish and plea for attention go unnoticed.

The imprisonment of wives in respectable
comfort draws Lardner's satire to a fine point. His
sympathy goes to the women; the men, whether
the Lou Greggs in the mansions or the Louis
Taylors in their houses, are villains. The women
are irrevocably stuck. They do not like Nora
Helmer, leave home or like Hedda Gabler, shoot
themselves or like Mrs. Alving, quietly run the
business. They are left to drink, solitaire, or death.
At the end of *Candide* when the old farmer pro-
claims that work saves men from vice, poverty,
and boredom, boredom may seem the least

threatening. For many women in Lardner's fiction, boredom rivals vice and poverty.

Characterized as late Edwardian and suited to an age of extended courtship and proper marriage, Lardner did not portray the fallen woman frequently in his fiction. Sex, for him, was not a subject for polite conversation nor a situation for fictional satire. However, he did include some immoral women whose explicit activities are assumed rather than detailed—Midge Kelly's friend Grace, Conrad Green's mistress Rose, and Hurry Kane's would-be mistress Evelyn.

Grace, in "Champion," is a kept woman, well dressed and well financed. While one hardly believes she attached herself to Midge Kelly with matrimony in mind, she does finally suggest it. Midge refuses by remembering for once his lawful wife, Emma. What becomes of Grace is another story. Midge discards her as he does other people when he finishes with their usefulness.

In "A Day with Conrad Green," (1925) the successful, semi-literate producer goes through an eventful day: his and his wife's names do not appear in the society page as expected; he decides not to attend his faithful secretary's funeral; his wife surprises him and to save face, he gives her pearls intended for his mistress, Rose. While the story focuses on Green and effectively treats the old theme of the deceiver deceived, Green's indiscrete behavior briefly introduces two questionable women. Joyce Brainard, wife of an international polo star, flirts with Green at a party. Excited over Green's theatrical power and prodded by several highballs, Joyce agrees to discuss her possible stage career in Green's office, a career she and Green "knew was impossible so long as Brainard lived." Things are left at an impasse until, the reader guesses, Brainard is disposed of.

The mistress Rose will play by Green's rules as long as he, too, keeps them. No lovemaking, she declares, until their business has been transacted. "Last time I saw you you insisted that I must give up everybody else but you. And I promised you it would be all off between Harry and I if—Well, you know. There was a little matter of some pearls." Green is a liar, a cheat, a thief; the women around him are greedy and self-serving, quite deserving the shabby treatment they get from him.

"Hurry Kane" (1927) gives wide range for Lardner's satirical attack: the talented, but slow-witted and greedy baseball rube, Elmer Kane, nicknamed "Hurry Kane"; ball players who can be bribed; and a glamorous woman who arranges a bribe. Convinced that the theatrical star Evelyn Cory likes him, Kane accepts the first installment of a $20,000 bribe. In truth, Evelyn "belongs to Sam Morris, the bookie," who has six to one odds on the game in question. Brought into the story to effect the exploitation of Kane, Evelyn is a static character, stereotyped by her good looks and her desire for money. Ironically, her questionable virtue looks innocent enough beside Kane who is temperatmental and self-centered, keeps a girl at home and one away from home, and neither returns the bribe nor throws the game.

Finally, in "Old Folks Christmas" (1929), Lardner lashes out at the bitter price people pay for making money. The parents, Tom and Grace, unwisely buy a ridiculous number of extravagant gifts for their children—a beaver coat, an opal ring, a roadster—only to find these gifts are declassé to Ted and Caroline who ask tactlessly if they can be exchanged. All the pleasure cherished with past Christmas times is gone since the children prefer going about with the younger set until all hours, are too tired to open presents at the accustomed time, and forget when Christmas dinner has always been served. Caroline (née Grace) may not be or may not become a fallen woman, but from Lardner's point of view, she displays the distressing characteristics of the modern generation. Out until four o'clock in the morning, Caroline finally comes in and her appearance draws a reaction from her parents.

"You look rumpled."

"They made me sit in the 'rumble' seat."

She laughed at her joke, said good night and went upstairs. She had not come even within handshaking distance of her father and mother.

"The Murdocks," said Tom, "must have great manners, making their guest ride in that uncomfortable seat."

Grace was silent.

In summing up Ring Lardner's attitude toward women, Donald Elder said, "He idealized women, and when he wrote of those who fell short of his ideal, the portraits were harsh and bitter. There are very few admirable women in all his stories; there are very few admirable men, either, but when women were coarse, egotistical or pretentious, they were much worse because he had expected them to be so much better."[3]

4

Players, Cheats, Spoil Sports

The most popular of Lardner's sports stories were the six he published in the *Saturday Evening Post* in 1914 that were later collected as *You Know Me Al* (1919). As Walton Patrick has pointed out, Lardner's famous rookie pitcher, Jack Keefe, first appeared on March 7, 1914, the day baseball fans greeted the Chicago White Sox and the New York Giants when they returned from a world tour. Coincidental or not, the timing was perfect. When Lardner abandoned Jack Keefe in 1919, he in many ways abandoned baseball: 1919 was the year eight Chicago White Sox players accepted bribes to throw the World Series. The decidedly inferior Cincinnati Reds won and Ring Lardner, who was covering the Series, lost more than his betting money. Among the eight who were indicted (the case was dismissed, but the eight players were barred from professional baseball for life) was Eddie Cicotte, a fine player whom Lardner liked and admired.[1] Lardner would cover many other World Series and would later return to baseball as subject matter in the six Danny Warner stories (1932), but after 1919 and after baseball became a batter's game, Lardner's passion for the sport diminished.[2]

The enthusiastic reception for the busher stories can be judged by the jump in Lardner's

payment from the *Post*—from $250 to $1500 a
story. The newspaper public was well aware of
Ring Lardner in 1914, but not until the mid-
twenties did he gain serious attention from literary
critics. When that attention came, Jack Keefe
rather surprisingly found an admirer in Virginia
Woolf. Today, Lardner scholars point to her 1925
essay, "American Fiction," and rightly so. She
who could not bring herself to read *Ulysses* read
the busher stories and said of Lardner, "With extraordinary ease and aptitude, with the quickest
strokes, the surest touch, the sharpest insight, he
lets Jack Keefe the baseball player cut out his own
outline, fill in his own depths, until the figure of
the foolish, boastful, innocent athlete lives before
us."[3]

Most frequently quoted from Woolf's essay is
her assessment of Lardner's interest in games: "It
has given him a clue, a centre, a meeting place for
the divers activities of people whom a vast
continent isolates, whom no tradition controls.
Games give him what society gives his English
brother."[4] In reality, for Lardner baseball did not
have a center that would always hold, a tradition
that would always remain.

In the teens and twenties, baseball was the
national pastime, unrivaled by the multiplicity of
sports teams that compete today for players and
ticket buyers. During his years traveling with both
the Chicago Cubs and the Chicago White Sox,
Ring Lardner produced hundreds of columns
about baseball. His knowledge of the sport itself
was extensive, and his friendships with players
were numerous. Dubbed "old owl eyes" by the
White Sox players, Lardner covered the games
and he also listened to the endless chatter that

helped fill the long hours of train travel from city to city. He thus knew the rules and the manager's strategy, the players and their skills, the gossip and the complaints. The reader familiar with baseball can appreciate the accuracy and finesse with which Lardner, through Jack Keefe, reports baseball plays in the busher stories of 1914.

The six stories of *You Know Me Al* demonstrate Lardner's expert knowledge of baseball. H. L. Mencken, in the *American Mercury*, said of these stories, "I doubt that anyone who is not familiar with professional ball players, intimately and at first hand, will ever comprehend the full merit of the amazing sketches in 'You Know Me, Al.'[5] Long regarded only as a baseball book, *You Know Me Al* has often been neglected by serious critics. Although "some of the baseball argot is dated," Donald Elder observes, "no one needs to know much about baseball terms to understand what Jack Keefe is talking about."[6]

Lardner's cynical view of the talented, but big-headed, athlete comes across clearly. The reader who will never try to keep a baseball score card has no difficulty seeing the brashness and bravado in Jack's excuses for his unsuccessful pitching. "Crawford got the luckiest three-base hit I ever see. He popped one way up in the air and the wind blowed it against the fence. At that Collins ought to of got it."

Jack's view of his pitching ability is akin to that of Philip Roth's pitcher, Gil Gamesh, who also has ready explanations for bad pitches. "If the umpire gave him a bad call he would be down off the mound breathing fire. 'You blind robber—it's a strike.'"[7] Although Gil's behavior on and off the baseball field is far worse than the inept ways of

Jack Keefe, *The Great American Novel* certainly
includes among its numerous literary echoes, Ring
Lardner's stories about Jack Keefe.

The language that Jack Keefe uses is a nota-
ble feature of these stories. His speech is not a re-
gional dialect understood by a few, but a language
as lasting as that of Huckleberry Finn's. Writing a
semiliterate Americanese (or *Ringlish*) in his letters to friend Al, Keefe's errors are legion.[8] They
reflect his paltry education and the fact that he
does not read anything; they do not, however,
keep the reader from understanding what he says.
Many critics have discussed the patterns of Keefe's
misspellings. *Comiskey, Cicotte, Pittsburg, Cincinnati,* for example, are spelled correctly because
these are words Jack would ask help with or
would see on hotel stationery. Errors occur in the
ordinary words he uses: *athaletes, takeing, ske-
dule, mistery, appresiated, vetrans, ernest, recruts.*
His sentences frequently contain verb errors: *have
went, have just ate, most of know, could of wrote,
have came.* Subjects and verbs and tenses do not
always agree: "Comiskey come back with an offer"; "He give it to me"; "that don't include my
meals"; "the papers says." Jack usually misuses
the pronoun in a compound expression: "I and
Florrie"; "him and I"; "her and I." Malapropisms abound—*spendrift* for spendthrift,
serious for series. Neither the plethora of grammatical errors nor the subject matter, however,
keeps the reader from quickly seeing Jack Keefe's
egotistical and biased attitude.

Baseball was the sport Lardner knew and
liked most; thus, it was a convenient and effective
vehicle for many stories. Donald Elder contends
that for Lardner, baseball represented "an ordered

world with definite rules of conduct"; to par-
ticipate, skill, integrity, and a code of honor were
required. Elder's theory is that Lardner's preoccupation "with sport reflected a longing for an ideal
world where the rules, if observed, guaranteed the
triumph of merit; it also reflected his acute sense
of the disparity between the way people were supposed to behave and the way they did."[9]

No evidence suggests that Lardner ever read
Johan Huizinga's 1930 study, *Homo Ludens,* that
interesting examination of the importance of play
as a cultural factor. However, Lardner's fiction
adds credence to Huizinga's premises. In discuss-
ing the characteristics of play, Huizinga says that
play creates "order, *is* order" and the least devia-
tion from that order "spoils the game . . . robs it of
its character and makes it worthless."[10] He notes
further that rules of games are absolutely binding;
but society, particularly archaic culture, is more
lenient to the cheat than to the spoil sport: the
former may be dishonest, but the latter shatters
the play.[11]

After seeing the first game of the 1919 World
Series, Lardner knew that a fix was on; he also
knew that the 1926 Jack Dempsey-Gene Tunney
prizefight "was a very well done fake, which lots
of us would like to say in print, but you know
what newspapers are where possible libel suits
are concerned."[12] Whether the players were
professional or amateur, whether the game was
baseball, prize-fighting, golf or bridge, Lardner's
characters pay little heed to the adage, it is not
whether you win or lose, but how you play the
game. (Huizinga refers to the popular Dutch saying, "It is not the marbles that matter, but the
game.") Fragile and selfish egos break rules, dis-

regard orders, alter scores; and their misdeeds make them into anti-athletes, anti-players. One further reference to Huizinga establishes the cultural phenomena of play and in turn shows how little regard Lardner's fictional athletes and players had for a game itself.

The arena, the card-table, the magic circle, the temple, the stage, the screen, the tennis court, the court of justice, etc., are all in form and function play-grounds, i.e. forbidden spots, isolated, hedged around, hallowed, within which special rules obtain. All are temporary worlds within the ordinary world, dedicated to the performance of an act apart.[13]

The 1920s regarded baseball as the national pastime and its players as heroes.[14] In spite of his love for the game, Lardner suffered no illusions about the players themselves. Like Jack Keefe, many had considerable natural talent, but they were not always intelligent nor did they deserve the fans' adulation. As Jonathan Yardley asserts, Lardner demythologized players, but did not debunk them; players were human beings with a full share of warts and shortcomings.

Jack Keefe is a spoil sport, far more concerned about himself than the game. Oblivious to the importance of order, he disregards training rules and threatens violence when he is criticized for disobeying the manager's orders during a game. Eating extra meals, he is overweight ("Hog-fat," the manager says); upset over something (usually women), he sneaks "down the street a ways and had a couple of beers before breakfast" or gets "a couple of highballs." Told to walk the next batter, Keefe throws a strike and the furious manager, he reports to Al, said "if I ever disobeyed his orders again he would suspend me without no pay and lick me too. Honest Al it was all I could do to keep from wrapping his jaw."

Jack Keefe is not Lardner's only example of the anti-athlete; Elmer "Hurry" Kane shares many of the same traits. Like Keefe, he eats too much. "Maybe I didn't tell you what an eater he was. Before Dave caught on to it, he was ordering one breakfast in his room and having another downstairs, and besides near choking himself to death at lunch and supper, he'd sneak out to some lunchroom before bedtime, put away a Hamburger steak and eggs and bring back three or four sandwiches to snap at during the night." Kane is an excellent pitcher and thus is looked after, humored, mollified, and praised by manager and players. In spite of himself, he wins ball games but his attitude is always the same—"I've got to look out for myself." The team members who placate him when he is lonesome for his girl in Yuma or when he finally realizes he has been the object of considerable kidding, do so because Kane's pitching means games won, and that, in turn, means money for them all.

Another spoil sport is Buster Elliott, the excellent batter in "My Roomy" (1914), who can hit the ball but will do nothing else. Playing in the outfield, he is supposed to go after and catch fly balls. "Why don't you go after these fly balls?" "Because I don't want 'em," says Elliott.[15] Always threatening to go home to his girl (whose letters he will not read), Elliott's bizarre behavior includes late-night antics—running the bathtub water all night long, shaving in the middle of the night, cutting on all the lights. He terrifies hotel guests by sending the elevator up and down until

women passengers faint. Pathological, Buster
Elliott nearly succeeds in killing his "girl" and her
husband by clubbing them with a baseball bat,
ironically the symbol of his sport and of his skill.

In these three athletes, Lardner embodies the
worst traits of the player. They have little use for
rules and no respect for order. They boast too
much and indulge themselves so that their interest in the game is in reality the praise and esteem
admirers give them, and the money they earn. As
critics have suggested, American baseball spectators would have expressed no surprise or disillusionment over the 1919 "Black Sox Scandal" if they had read Ring Lardner's stories about
baseball players. He had clearly shown that the
baseball heroes were just men, and not always
smart or good ones at that. Egotistical, self-indul-
gent, unintelligent—in many cases, their own
interests, not the orderly game, took precedence.

While early baseball may have counted men
on the teams who bore some resemblance to Jack
Keefe, he should not be regarded as the typical
baseball player. Throughout the Keefe stories, as
well as in his column, "In the Wake of the
News," Lardner introduced real baseball players
who generally represented experience, common
sense, and regard for order. Today their names are
familiar but to a few; however, to the baseball en-
thusiast of the twenties, those names were impressive—Kid Gleason (used throughout the
stories in *You Know Me Al*), Frank Chance
(handsome and intelligent player-manager of the
Chicago Cubs),Frank Schulte, Eddie Collins.
These and other respected players enter and strike
a balance to the Jack Keefes, the Hurry Kanes,
and the Buster Elliotts. Baseball in the teens and

twenties may not have been a widely respected profession and it may have counted tobacco-chewing, whiskey-drinking, poker-playing men among its regulars; nevertheless, between the myths of the hero and the fool were competent athletes who played the game and played it well.

Lardner's fictional baseball players were then not the ideal, the hero, as an anecdote in Jonathan Yardley's biography bears out. "As was the custom in baseball's early years, the White Sox were capitalizing on their success by making a barnstorming tour of the provinces. The small Wisconsin town in question awaited their visit with all the excitement due a papal audience, and when their train pulled in, a little boy rushed up to see his heroes. He looked, then turned and said, 'Why they're only *men,* aren't they?'" This anecdote and much of Lardner's fiction illustrate Louis Rubin's assertion in "The Great American Joke" that "between what men would be and must be, as acted out in American experience, has come much pathos, no small amount of tragedy, and also a great deal of humor."[16]

Lardner's criticism extended to baseball spectators, many of whom claimed an intimate knowledge of players and strategy when, in fact, they knew and understood little. In "Oddities of Bleacher 'Bugs,'" which appeared in the Boston *American* in 1911, Lardner distinguished the real baseball fan ("Who knows the players are just people") from the baseball bug ("Who knows most of the players by sight, as they appear on the field, but wouldn't know more than one or two of them if he saw them on the street"). The bleacher bug tries to judge everything he sees but "thinks something is a bonehead play when it is really

good, clever baseball . . . He must talk unhesi-
tantly, as if he had all the facts, and never stam-
mer or back up when his assertions are ques-
tioned." Pretense in players and spectators alike
drew Lardner's scorn.

Golf and bridge are the games that Lardner's
non-professional players engage in most often.
Many of them, like Stuart and Rita Johnston in
"Reunion" (1925), take the games seriously. Having finally shot an 85, Stuart squirms throughout
the story to get to the golf course; Rita counts the
day lost that does not include a bridge game "with
its twenty or thirty rubbers." The Long Island
Johnstons' games are temporarily thwarted by
houseguests from Niles, Michigan (Rita's brother
and his wife), and a reunion after twenty years.
Bob and Jennie talk about their vegetable garden
and folks from Niles, bemoan the absence of a
radio, and long to compare the New York version
of "Abie's Irish Rose" with the Chicago production which they saw three times. Neither couple
shares the other's interests and each prepares a lie
to cut short the visit. The Masons tell their lie first
and flee to New York for sight seeing and one
show ("Abie's Irish Rose," of course), delighted to
be rid of suggestions to play games they have never
taken up.

Social distinctions in the story are sharply
marked. The Masons bring few clothes (one
suitcase, no trunk), their grammar is flawed ("We
didn't bring no trunks"), they adore the radio
("We had Omaha one night"), they do not like
the movies, and they neither smoke nor drink. Jennie picks up *May Fair* and asks if it is good, but
she has never heard of its author Michael Arlen,

or his famous novel, *The Green Hat.* Rita, of course, is an Arlen admirer. Most important, the Masons do not know any of the games that delight the elite of Long Island. To the Johnstons, they are small-town hicks, liking simple-minded pleasures—gardens, radio programs, and restoring the family homeplace. Unable to appreciate or admire the glories of the Johnston home at Sands Point, Long Island ("Bob walked around the yard and plotted the changes he would make if it were his"), Bob and Jennie bore their in-laws and, ironically, are bored by them.

Ring Lardner, himself at home in Niles, Michigan, and in Long Island, presents the small-town couple as limited, but sensible. They are unpretentious, clean-living, loyal—good country people. The suburbanites are less gently treated. Expert in games they may be, but when the Johnstons are bereft of playing these games to entertain themselves (and whoever else is around), they have no other recourse. Stuart survives the visit by drinking—seven highballs with his meal—and Rita does not want to be left alone with her own relatives. No talk of the past interests her and she does not care if she never sees the homeplace again. Lardner, who was extremely close to his own family as Ellis was to hers, had little sympathy for this suburban couple.

As much as Ring Lardner worked to provide his family with the affluent surroundings of prestigious Long Island living, he saw through the crudeness of new money and the hedonistic madness that the twenties nurtured. He may have left the Midwest and come East, but he never disdained the small town back home. Nowhere does he make his feelings about the wealthy Long Is-

land life clearer than in "Reunion." Here he portrays Gatsby's valley of ashes. "The road leading
from New York to the town of Long Island's north
shore is for the most part, as scenically attractive
as an incincerating plant. Nevertheless, Jennie
kept saying, 'How beautiful!' and asking Rita who
were the owners of various places which looked as
if they had been disowned for many years."

"Contract" (1929), "Three Without Doubled" (1917), and "Who Dealt?" (1926) differ
radically in tone, but contract bridge is a controlling factor in each. A thorough knowledge of bridge
is tantamount to understanding these stories completely; however, the irritating and fatuous
characters emerge clearly even if one does not
know that "Three Without Doubled" means that
the bid contracted was three no-trump and that
the opposition challenged the bid by doubling. If
the player fails to make his contract, the opposition gets the penalty points, doubled. An excellent
bridge player himself, Lardner added an author's
postscript to "Contract," a word to his own bridge
partners. "This story won't get me anything but
the money I am paid for it. Even if it be read by
those with whom I usually play—Mr. C., Mrs.
W., Mr. T., Mrs. R. and the rest—they will think
I mean two other fellows and tear into me like
wolves next time I bid a slam and make one odd."

The spoil sport works away in these three
stories; out of sheer ignorance, the player-narra-
tors shatter each game. None of these games are
for pleasure, but for gaining the highest number of
points and winning a prize. When a novice player
blunders, quick and caustic criticism follows.

"Three Without Doubled," one of the five
stories of Gullible and the Missus (collected under

the title, *Gullible's Travels,* 1917), treats bridge as a means of social advancement. Invited to replace a couple in the weekly neighborhood bridge elite, the Missus happily accepts. The husband, a non-player, refers to the venture as "our latest plunge in the cesspool o'society." The husband's objection to accepting the invitation is a serious one: "How am I goin' to get by at a bridge party when I haven't no idear how many cards to deal?" He would prefer "pedro or five hundred or rummy, or somethin' that you don't need no college course in," but the wife is adamant. "They's only just the one game that Society plays, and that's bridge. Them other games is jokes."

Frantic attempts to learn bridge fail. Their old friends, the Hatches, are good enough to coach them, but not to be told about the exclusive group. Predictably, the husband's mistakes and his wise-cracks spoil the game and the dispositions of the other players. In the end, the Hatches have been invited to replace the rejected Gullibles. Had Gullible and the Missus mastered the game, they could have taken, for them, a social step forward; but the husband not only does not know the rules, he remains flippant and rude toward those who take the game seriously.

Much like "Three Without Doubled," "Contract" has a player ignorant of the rules. One of Lardner's suburban stories, "Contract" is narrated by Shelton, a New York magazine publisher, whose wife is sure "suburbanites would be less tedious and unattractive" than city people. The husband makes a valiant, but disastrous, attempt to be more sociable. His thesis—"It's a conviction of most bridge players and some golf players, that God sent them into the world to teach"—is borne

out as his bridge partner points out his every error. These people are nouveau riche, Shelton finally learns, and thus now less attractive socially.
Revenge comes at the bridge dinner the next week
when the castigated bridge novice, Shelton,
meticulously corrects the table manners, grammar,
and diction of the group, easily extricating himself
and his wife from the weekly commitment. Now
invited to play bridge with *real* society, Shelton is
abashed to find that his thesis still holds true. At
the end of the first hand, his partner hisses across
the card table, "*Why* didn't you lead me a club?
You *must* watch the discards."

"Who Dealt?," a brilliant monologue, takes
place at the bridge table where a new wife reveals
all the private secrets, trivial and serious, of her
husband's life. Intermittently, her exposé is suspended while she ineptly tries to pay attention to
the game. The bridge buff is amused and appalled
when she gives this response to her husband's bid
of no-trump.

Let me see; I wish I knew what to do. I haven't any
five-card—it's terrible. Just a minute. I wish somebody
could—I know I ought to take—but—well, I'll pass.
Oh, Tom, this is the worst you ever saw, but I don't
know what I could have done.[The game ends with
Tom two tricks shy of his bid.] . . . Oh, Tom, only two
down? Why, I think you did splendidly! I gave you a
miserable hand and Helen had—what didn't you have,
Helen? You had the ace, king of clubs. No, Tom had
the king. No, Tom had the queen. Or was it spades?
And you had the ace of hearts. No, Tom had that. No,
he didn't. What *did* you have, Tom? I don't exactly see
what you bid on. Of course I was terrible, but—what's
the difference anyway?

Ideally, the bridge player keeps track of all fifty-
two cards, watching and anticipating each play.

The wife has botched every hand and has also laid her husband's life down on the table to his chagrin and embarrassment. As the story ends, Tom is off the wagon.

Two of Lardner's golf stories, "Mr. Frisbie" (1928) and "A Caddy's Diary" (1922) portray the cheating golfer. Mr. Frisbie, a wealthy and cantankerous man, plays alone on his eighteen-hole course. His chauffeur is his caddy and reliably doctors the score. If Mr. Frisbie plays well, he is amiable; if not, his family can expect no favors. The climax of the slight and somewhat contrived plot makes Mr. Frisbie akin to Molière's Orgon and Gorgibus: he senselessly insists his daughter give up the man she loves and marry his choice, rich Junior Holt. The all-knowing chauffeur arranges a golf match and Holt is carefully set up to officiously correct Mr. Frisbie's game. Holt, a fine golfer, spoils the day, infuriating Mr. Frisbie with his superiority. Holt, of course, loses the bride.

In "A Caddy's Diary," Lardner explores the price for which people will sell their honest nature—for a paltry golf club tournament prize or for a one-dollar tip. Cheating on the course is conveniently overlooked: strokes are miscounted and balls are surreptitiously moved from roughs, thrown across brooks, kicked from sandtraps. Under the guise of a gentleman's game, corruption runs high on the golf course. No one cares as long as his score card bears a decent figure or his pockets hold sufficient tips.

Midge Kelly in "Champion" throws a fight for eighty dollars; "Hurry" Kane does not throw a baseball game, but he says he will and keeps the five-thousand-dollar installment of a large bribe; pitchers hide their mistakes with alibis; golfers lie about their scores; some bridge players do not even learn the rules while others covet points and prizes.

A baseball reporter by trade, an avid golfer, bridge, and poker player, Lardner naturally turned to sports when he wrote fiction. When he did, his fictitious players are not heroes and they do not command respect; they are petty and self-serving from the baseball diamond to the parlor bridge table. The spoil sports ruin the play, the cheats demean the player. Above such immature and common behavior, Lardner satirizes these players and leaves the reader and himself removed and aloof. The conditions under which cheats and spoil sports thrive render the sport pointless and absurd. Lardner's view bears kinship to Huizinga's anecdote in *Homo Ludens* about the Shah of Persia who on a visit to England "is supposed to have declined the pleasure of attending a race meeting, saying he knew very well that one horse runs faster than another."[17] With that predisposed mind, pointless indeed to attend, and pointless to enter into games that are bound by rules and centered in order when participants cheat and spoil.

5

Humor of Disenchantment

Constance Rourke in her 1931 study *American Humor* stated that all of Lardner's stories "turn on humor; practical jokes make the substance of many situations as in an earlier day, but in the end the brutality which underlies them is exposed."[1] Rourke's early assessment appeared before "Mamma" and "Second-Act Curtain" were well known, stories Jonathan Yardley calls "noteworthy as the first of the 'dark' fiction he would try his hand at off and on for the rest of his writing career."[2] It is true that much of Lardner's fiction in the last years of his life is "dark," reflecting his severely deteriorating health and his uncertain finances. The narrators in "Large Coffee" (1929) and "Second-Act Curtain" (1930), as Lardner frequently did, retreat to a New York City hotel room to work, isolating themselves because they can not be "where everybody else was having a good time." Such real and fictional conditions understandably produced "dark" fiction.

Rourke's judgment, however, points to all of Lardner's fiction which does indeed *turn on humor,* but does in the end expose the brutality underneath. As we have seen, Lardner's 1914 Busher stories amused thousands (the illustrations alone that the *Saturday Evening Post* carried with them ensured the comic tone). Yet Jack Keefe's funny antics and bumbling ways do not cancel his insensitivity and his disregard for order and decorum. What is present in Lardner's fiction may be described as black humor, from the heartless practical joker in "The Maysville Minstrel" and "Haircut" to the bewildering nurse in "Zone of Quiet" to the chaotic scenes of the nonsense plays to the grimly humorous treatment of mental distress and death in the late works.

In his essay, "The Mode of Black Humor," Brom Weber points to the contrast between the comic tradition of Anglo-American culture which viewed humor as intrinsically good-natured, trivial, kindly; and the unpredictable, topsy-turvy, often hostile and sadistic character of black humor [which] may well appear to be perverse and intolerable."[3] Although black humor leaped into prominence between 1955–1965 as if it had never been a part of American literature, Weber notes that its characteristics have found expression throughout our literature; and these characteristics are prominent in Lardner's fiction.

Weber sees black humor deriving "from its rejection of morality and other human codes ensuring earthly pattern and order, from its readiness to joke about the horror, violence, injustice, and death that rouses its indignation, from its avoidance of sentimentality by means of emotional coolness, and from its predilection for surprise and shock."[4] Real literary merit has often been condemned because it presented such crude and brutal humor. Certainly critics have emphasized Lardner's bleak outlook, qualifying his position as a great humorist by documenting the extent of his bitter nature.

Mencken's 1926 review of *The Love Nest and Other Stories,* entitled "A Humorist Shows His Teeth," found no clowning in "Haircut,"

"Zone of Quiet," and "Rhythm." These stories
were "satire of the most acid and appalling sort—
satire wholly removed, like Swift's before it, from
the least weakness of amiability, or even pity."[5]
Clifton Fadiman called his 1929 review of *Round
Up,* "Pitiless Satire," and charged Lardner with
exhibiting excessive hatred. "Mr. Lardner has
also been praised as a humorous writer. He is
popularly supposed to be a funny man. If these
collected stories do not absolutely give the lie to
this conception, they at least tend to modify it
greatly . . . Mr. Lardner is the deadliest because
the coldest of American writers. Unlike Sinclair
Lewis, he is without a soft streak."[6]

Fadiman further charged that Lardner hated
his characters and continued this theme in a 1933
essay, "Ring Lardner and the Triangle of Hate,"
in the *Nation.* "The special force of Ring
Lardner's work springs from a single fact: he just
doesn't like people. Except Swift, no writer has
gone farther on hatred alone."[7] Fadiman alludes
to Lardner's "icy satiric power" and claims that
the blackness of the American middle class has
entered his soul. With a devastating biblical allusion, Fadiman removes all vestiges of Lardner's
humor. "Read beneath the lines and you will see
that everything he meets or touches drives him into
a cold frenzy, leaving him without faith, hope, or
charity."[8] This grim assessment came in 1933, the
year Lardner was forty-eight and the year he died.

Later critics have not echoed Fadiman's judgment completely, but even the titles of some recent
Lardner studies indicate that critics still share
Fadiman's views to some extent. Louis Hasley
published "Ring Lardner: The Ashes of Idealism"; Forrest L. Ingram, "Fun at the Incinerating

Plant: Lardner's Wry Wasteland"; and Norris
Yates, "The Isolated Man of Ring Lardner."
Walter Blair and Hamlin Hill see Lardner's sardonic vernacular in his early stories as "a weapon
for depicting the stupidity and insensitivity of rural
folk" and declare that his "later humor was in the
dead center of the lunatic fringe."[9] Strong state-
ments indeed about a man persistently identified
as a humorist.

The 1920s ushered in an era of crisis, one
particularly conducive for the production of black
humor; and that literary approach, as Brom
Weber points out, had "little respect for the values
and patterns of thought, feeling, and behavior that
had kept Anglo-American culture stable and effective, have provided a basis of equilibrium for society and the individual."[10] The 1919 Volstead
Act forbade the sale of alcoholic beverages, but
drinking in America flourished as never before.
The time of speakeasies and bathtub gin brought
with it the surge of bootleggers and organized
crime. Staid, Victorian mores that had upheld
tradition and authority dissolved in the wake of
mass-produced automobiles, short-skirted and bob-
haired flappers, and stock-market fortunes.

As the twenties witnessed the mushrooming
of the stock market, Lardner saw his own financial
state soar. He was writing a "Weekly Letter" and
the comic strip for the Bell Syndicate which gave
him "a cushion of nearly $50,000 a year before he
began piling short-story income on top of it—and
within five years he was getting as much as $4,500
for a single story . . . His income eventually would
rise to the neighborhood of $100,000 from writing
alone . . . the approximate equivalent of a late-se-
venties income of $500,000."[11] Yet he had the

haunting memory of the speculations that ruined his father's fortune, and the fear of not adequately providing for his own family, a reality the 1930s brought to him and countless Americans after the stock market crashed.

While Lardner clearly rode the affluent wave of the early twenties, the flurry of the Jazz Age, the social corruption surrounding Prohibition, the proliferation of expatriots in that lost generation offered characters who were evil, sadistic, pathetic, and insensitive. Lardner indulged in, yet scorned, the garish life of his nouveau riche neighbors in Great Neck, Long Island, whose houses might have been taken, he once wrote, for the Yale Bowl. On the other hand, the horror and boredom of ordinary middle-class life occupied much of his fiction and "turned him from gentle humor to Swiftian satire."[12] Sinclair Lewis and Thomas Wolfe, in their different ways, were also voicing displeasure over the small-town obsession with progress and the middle-class citizen's dedication to material success.

Frequently, Lardner's characters are themselves perverse and intolerable or are innocent characters forced into perverse and intolerable situations. With few exceptions, the characters are isolated and alienated from meaningful and happy experiences. Jonas Spatz suggests that "in a real sense, this isolation was always Lardner's subject."[13] Norris Yates points to a key factor when he says "Lardner's characters talk a lot, but their preoccupation with self frustrates their efforts at communication."[14] Such characters and situations occupy Lardner's stories that manifest black humor.

In spite of the bleakness surrounding both

characters and subject matter, Lardner could still be quite funny. For instance, Booth, the song writer in "Second-Act Curtain," treats the reading material left in his hotel room with comic disrespect. Dismissed is "Heart Throbs, a collection . . . of favorite bits of verse or prose of well-known Americans; Holy Bible, anonymous, but a palpable steal of Gideon's novel of the same name, and the Insidious Dr. Fu Manchu by Sax Rohmer." The last title about "the insidious chink" was so bad that the narrator declared, "It is all right for a guest to bring a book like this with him, but there certainly ought to be a penalty for leaving it in the room." Further, Booth points out the inadequacy of the biblical narrative and the insipidness of that treasured verse of sentimentality, "Home, Sweet Home."

Holy Bible began too slow and after another powder Booth dived into Heart Throbs, only to be confronted by the complete text of Home, Sweet Home. Now out in the town where Booth's family was spending the summer the natives had pointed with pride to the house where Mr. Payne, who wrote this famous lyric, used to live. If the natives had ever read the whole thing, they probably would have burned the house instead of point to it.

Deaths, funerals, and physical handicaps are serious topics that black humor may violate without restraint or conscience. Lardner, who could not bear to see suffering in humans or in animals, surprisingly bypasses the normally somber reaction to death. Two examples from *The Big Town* show an extreme emotional coolness toward death.

Kate, the husband-hunter, has not been reduced to "a vale of tears" upon hearing that her

aviator-suitor has died in a crash which spilled
"him and his invention . . . all over Long Island."
Kate's calm, sensible reaction precluded shock and
grief. Her sister Ella explains. "She says if that
could of happened, why the invention couldn't of
been no good after all. And the Williams probably
wouldn't of give him a plugged dime for it."
Jimmy Ralston of the Follies, a second-rate
comedian Kate does marry, figures in a macabre
scene where family deaths are callously discussed.

"Is your mother living?" Kate ast him.

"No," he says. "She was killed in a railroad wreck. I'll
never forget when I had to go and identify her. You
wouldn't believe a person could get that mangled?"
"No," he says, "my family's all gone. I never seen my
father. He was in the pesthouse with smallpox when I
was born and he died there. And my only sister died of
jaundice. I can still—"

But Kate was scared we'd wake up the hotel, laughing,
so she says: "Do you ever give imitations?"

Lardner's burlesque autobiography, *The
Story of a Wonder Man* (1927) reports a few of
the pranks he and other participants played in
Polyandry Hospital, Hallowe'en, 1896. No explanation could soften the cruelty here. "The patient
in Room 18 had been almost fatally burned in an
apartment house fire. A crowd of twenty other
patients and nurses gathered outside his door and
yelled, 'Fire!' till he jumped out the window. As
Room 18 was on the fifth floor, you can imagine
his surprise."

The characters in "Dinner Bridge" (1927),
one of Lardner's nonsense plays, stay busy tearing
up the Fifty-ninth Street Bridge to hunt a lost
cigar and to recount their aberrant acts. Taylor, a

Negro laborer, has made a habit of stopping funeral processions on the bridge and getting mourners attached to the wrong hearse. "It generally always winds up with the friends and relations of the late Mr. Cohen attending the final obsequies of Mrs. Levinsky." The other laborers agree, in unison, that "Taylor has a great time with the funerals."

Act 5 of "Taxidea Americana" (1924), another nonsense play, takes place at Camp Randall just before the annual game between Wisconsin and the Wilmerding School for the Blind. Two sets of stage directions and a cheer-song from each school comprise the act. The Wisconsin song smacks of conventional football cheer rhetoric with a mangled line from Auld Lang Syne thrown in.

Far above Cayuga's waters with its waves of blue,
On Wisconsin, Minnesota and Bully for old Purdue.
Notre Dame, we yield to thee! Ohio State, Hurrah!
We'll drink a cup o' kindness yet in praise of auld
    Nassau!

The reader is left puzzled about who is cheering whom, but the Wilmerding rooters applaud the Wisconsin performance and then take their turn, shocking the reader with this incongruous song.

We are always there on time!
We are the Wilmerding School for the Blind!
Better backfield, better line!
We are the Wilmerding School for the Blind!
Yea!

Nothing light-hearted, funny, amusing, or laughter-arousing emerges in "Large Coffee" (1929), "Mama" (1930), and "Poodle" (1934), stories representative of black humor in every

aspect of the narrative, not just in an occasional
episode. "Large Coffee" is *almost* purely humorous as the narrator describes his difficulty with
hotel room service. All he wants is an order of four
cups of coffee for one person, but in spite of
describing the order in every conceivably clear
way, he ends up with two place settings, two
cereal bowls, and two plates of bacon and eggs
along with two servings of coffee. Man against the
system can produce amusing frustrations, but
"Large Coffee" places its humor in the improper
conduct of some hotel tenants, in the obtuseness of
the hotel staff, and in the frustration of the principal character, a Mr. Lardner who checked into a
hotel to escape the distraction caused by the
knowledge "that other people were having fun."

His pleas for "large coffee" go unheeded and
a two-week silence leads the insensitive chamber-
maids to conclude that he "would need a clean
towel if living, and perhaps two of them, if dead."
Dead he is, "his head crushed in by a blow from
some blunt instrument, probably another hotel."
Absurd details do not diminish the maddening and
fatal frustration of not being listened to.

Mamma, a thirty-year-old woman "who
would have been rather pretty if she had had more
color and had not looked so tired," had ridden the
crosstown car from Broadway to the end of the
line. Her presence puzzles the trainmen who begin
a brief exchange with her. Short questions and
answers reveal their incapacity to understand her
distress, guessing instead that she is pickled, crazy,
or a hophead.

Escorted and left in Grand Central Station,
Mamma next answers a policeman's questions
with childish replies.

"Do you live in the city?"

"I think so."

"What's your name?"

"My name? My name's Mamma."

"What's your last name?" asked the policeman.

"That's all—just Mamma."

"What's your husband's name?"

"Dad. He's at the office, but he'll stop for me, pretty soon, I hope. I must get home and bake a cake."

The Travelers' Aid Guest House for a night brings no improvement so the city hospital's psychopathic ward follows. Here, questions are numerous. Mamma accuses the nurses of nagging her, but volunteers longer answers about Dad and Brother and Betty. No address comes to her, no one makes inquiries about her, and police fail to find the alleged family. "The psychopathic ward was beginning to regard her as part of its permanent equipment. And then—suddenly she recalled her other name . . . 'What is that you're saying? Is it your name?' 'Yes. That's it— Carns.'"

The surname leads to the discovery that Dad, Brother, and Betty all died two months ago from flu, that Mamma left the apartment owing rent and creditors, and that contrary to her claim to the nurses, "she herself was the most useless, helpless woman you ever seen in a sick room." Unable to confront Mamma with the grim reality of her life, the nurse claims the telephone book lists no Carns and Mamma is content to have gotten the name wrong and to wait until Dad comes along to get her.

Basic incongruity prevails. The woman is young, not old and helpless; her life had been happy, if improvident ("He makes a good salary, but we haven't saved. We have too much fun, I guess"); names have no full identity beyond family relationships. The story fails to come full circle and leaves Mamma as part of the permanent equipment of the psychopathic ward—another "thing"—to endlessly wait for a husband who will not appear.

While Lardner does not suggest here that mental illness is a cause for frivolity, the trainmen found Mamma's behavior peculiar and to a degree humorous. On one level, Mamma's answers to the nurse create humor as her report of the illness illustrates—the joke, she thinks, was on the doctor.

"Who are Brother and Betty?"

"Why do you ask so many questions?"

"I'm interested in you," said Miss Fraser.

"Well, Brother is my little boy, and Betty is my little girl. They both had the flu. And Dad had it. And Doctor was frightened. He thought they were all going to die. But we fooled him. They all got well."

Protected by her mental block, Mamma will continue to give the same answers to the same questions as long as her artificial reality lasts.

The nameless narrator in "Poodle," Waldron's best and most valuable employee, first faces the absence of his annual Christmas bonus, then the hope of a raise which does not appear. A dismissal notice does. His wife, Mary, is a typical Lardner woman. Thoughtless and a spendthrift, she takes his check "and went ahead and spent it whatever way she wanted to, which was to help pay for a new car because the one she bought last year had cigaret ashes on the running board." She is, of course, furious over the missing bonus and threatens lawsuits.

When the narrator says his wife "can outgloat any two women I ever met, and doesn't need to speak a word," he describes her chief characteristic. When their closest friends, the Ingrams, come for a last visit (he has been fired and they must move away), the narrator takes an extra drink and tells Mary about the proposed raise. That information "put her in a position to send her best friend away thoroughly whipped."

Unable to tell his wife he has been fired, the narrator goes to the city as usual and unsuccessfully hunts work. Before his time and money run out, he is claimed by Phil Hughes, a wealthy deranged man with hospital out-patient privileges if a companion will control his lavish and erratic spending. Convinced that the narrator is Ben "Poodle" Collins from back home in Oconomowoc, Hughes engages him in conversation. Their talk reveals Hughes to be kind, affable, harmless; the narrator is sardonic, cynical.

"Listen, Cuckoo," I said, "you've got me mixed up with some other dog. You and I are strangers," I said, "and it suits me fine to continue the relationship." . . .

"I'm not crazy, Poodle," he said, "but I *am* under observation."

"Why not?" I said, "You're talking as loud as a Congressman, and even sillier."

Dr. Gregory verifies the narrator's references and the former most valuable employee at Waldron's becomes "a seventy-two-hundred dollar day nurse named Poodle. I spend eight hours a day with a crazy person that pays me and the rest of the time with one that doesn't." Defeated and dehumanized, the narrator accepts his lot.

A wealthy mental patient, a shrewish and gloating wife, a successful young working man turned "Poodle," and a young woman now alone and alienated from reality are elements that provide dark humor. Not judged one of his most successful stories, "Poodle" caused Lardner much bitterness as he revealed in a February 3, 1933, letter to Max Perkins. Seriously ill, Lardner was enroute to California as his doctor had ordered, "to be gone," he wrote Perkins, "till the money has disappeared." His letter closes on a note of despair symbolized in the story "Poodle" which had been rejected by the *Saturday Evening Post, Collier's,* and the *American Mercury.*

This letter doesn't seem to be properly constructed or quite clear. That is a symptom of my state of mind, but the fact that I can laugh at the succession of turn-downs of a story which everybody but the *Post* has had a kind word for but no inclination to buy, makes me hopeful for the future. Maybe some day I can write a piece about the story's Cook's tour—it is the first one I ever wrote that wasn't accepted by the first or second publication to which it was offered, and that either means go west old man or quit writing fiction or both.

Lardner obviously was not laughing at the succession of turn-downs by publishers any more than the characters in these stories of black humor laugh at their sad or ridiculous lots. All have become disenchanted since jobs, health, or family are gone. Yet incongruous situations, amusing dialogue, and unexpected events do evoke some laughter from subjects that generally are considered too serious for laughter, too bitter for frivolity.

6

The Would-Be Songsmith

Music and the theater, along with baseball, were Lardner's greatest interests. His parents' household in Niles, Michigan, had a pipe organ and two pianos; various family members were installed in the choir or at the organ of the Episcopal Church. The Niles Opera House mounted several modest, but well-received, productions including a two-act comedy, *Zanzibar,* for which Lardner wrote the music and most of the lyrics and in which he acted and sang. Apparently, the enthusiastic reception was confined to the 1903 Niles production. Ring Lardner, Jr. hints that the popularity was justifiably limited. "I have never heard the music, but I have read the book [Harry Schmidt's] and lyrics, and the best I can say for the defense is that the lyrics stand up a little better than the book."[1] Lardner family musicales in Niles were frequent and Ring Lardner's own four sons staged their musical extravaganzas in Great Neck. John's masterpiece at age fourteen was an American version of *H.M.S. Pinafore* called *U.S.S. Skinafore,* a shade more complicated than the simple parody Jim and Ring, Jr. concocted, "Yes we have no pajamas, We have no pajamas tonight."

Like his mother, Lardner had perfect pitch and besides the piano, taught himself to play a half-dozen musical instruments, Christmas gifts from Ellis over the years. During much of the free

time on the long baseball trips, Lardner wrote
songs and tried to get actors in musical comedies to
sing them. Jonathan Yardley does not exaggerate
the matter when he says Lardner "never had any
success worth serious mention, but he attempted to
write songs for the rest of his life and there is
absolutely no question that he would have thrown
over his entire literary/journalistic career in a split
second had the chance arisen to make a living as a
'songsmith.'"[2]

An early attempt was a 1908 collaboration
with Doc White called "Little Puff of Smoke,
Good Night," a sentimental lullabye sung by a
Negro mother. This song did earn some royalties
which Lardner referred to in a letter to Ellis
detailing the money the couple would have when
they married. "There'll be a pay-day on 'Little
Puff of Smoke' in July and perhaps something
from other things some time. These can be used in
helping pay for the piano."[3] These royalties,
however, fell short of the piano price since almost
all of Mr. Abbott's $300 wedding gift went to buy
one, "Ring solemnly promising that the bank account would be repaid from what was rapidly becoming the household chimera, 'song money.'"[4]

Other songs followed, but none earned
enough profit to make Lardner a full-time
songsmith. Although Lardner and White's "Gee,
It's a Wonderful Game," was sung in the Chicago
ball park, it could not supplant Norworth and von
Tilzer's still familiar, "Take Me Out to the Ball
Game," introduced the year before.

Two songs in 1916 are of passing interest.
One, a poorly-timed tribute to "Oh! Mister Theo-
dore," had words by Lee S. Roberts and music by
Ring Lardner. Three chorus lines illustrate the

hackneyed quality—"We're tired of being goats /
We'll give you all our votes / For Teddy, you're a
bear."[5] "Old Billy Baker" had music by Jerome
Kern, a song writer Lardner greatly admired.
Yardley suggests that the Lardner song Bert
Williams sang in the 1917 Follies was "Home,
Sweet Home (That's Where the Real War Is),"
but no copy is extant. Lardner counted the Negro
singer, Bert Williams, among his life-long friends.
Finally, Lardner countered his naive expectation
that Prohibition would stop his chronic drinking
with two songs bemoaning the passage of the
Volstead Act, "Prohibition Blues" (1918) and
"Toledo Blues" (1919).

Elder finds it impossible to ascertain exactly
how many lyrics Lardner did write. Of the dozen
that were published, none maintained any popularity among American songs and today the titles
are altogether unfamiliar. His theatrical experience followed much the same line. Morris Gest
paid him $3,000 for the rights to his plays and
musical comedies, an arrangement which suggests
Lardner's potential. Gest, it turned out, made an
unwise investment.

Lardner's life-long theatrical ambitions met
with little success. In addition to the brief
nonsense plays, he worked on several musical
shows that were never produced and on a few that
were. The best discussion of Lardner's dramatic
attempts remains Donald Elder's 1956 study, *Ring
Lardner, A Biography,* which points out Lardner's talent in turning out lyrics and devising
plots, but his failure in dealing with theater
production and temperamental actors.

The unproduced work deserved mention since
it documents the aborted attempts Lardner made.

With Gene Buck, Lardner attempted to write a
show that Flo Ziegfeld wanted for Fanny Brice,
but as Elder notes, when Ziegfeld hired "professional writers" to rewrite the script, Lardner abandoned the project. He and Buck also
worked on a musical adaption of *Gullible's
Travels* to be called *Going South*. Again Ziegfeld interposed, this time so altering the main
characters that Lardner's basic satire was oblit-
erated. Disregarding Buck's urgings, Lardner
refused to sign Ziegfeld's contract and in a letter to
Scott Fitzgerald vented his exasperation. "I've got
a story coming out in 'Liberty' for October 3
[1925, "A Day with Conrad Green"] of which
Flo is the hero. When, and if, he reads it, he won't
offer me any more contracts, even lousy ones."[6]
Later, he did reconsider, but the resulting working
conditions with Buck, Ziegfeld, and Vincent Youmans fell into general confusion.

Also unproduced was Lardner's version of
Offenbach's witty *Orpheus in the Underworld*
which portrayed Orpheus as a Tin Pan Alley
songwriter tune-thief, Eurydice as the long-suf-
fering wife who gets free to marry a prince, and
the Olympian deities as low comedy characters.
Although Lardner's lyrics showed considerable ingenuity, the whole work, Elder comments, was
little more than a hodge-podge. Lardner turned
again to opera with an updated version of
Carmen. Set in Jazz Age Long Island and populated by bootleggers and flappers, it never reached
the stage although Yardley says a private production occurred in 1976. (Another interesting treatment of *Carmen,* of course, is Oscar Hammerstein
II's *Carmen Jones,* 1943, which moved the plot
from Seville to a southern parachute factory dur-

ing World War II.) A modernization of "Cin-
derella," set in Long Island, featured the Prince of
Wales as the prince and "just another Mildred
Miller" as the heroine. In spite of some promising
dialogue and lyrics, producers rejected it and
Lardner's attempt came to nothing.

Elder calls *All at Sea* "the most professional
and the cleverest of the musical comedies that Ring
worked on."[7] A 1928 collaboration with Paul
Lannin, *All at Sea* takes place on a round-the-
world cruise with action centering on a gangster in
"a mock-lugubrious song meant to be sung by a
man with a deep voice and a solemn, expression-
less face (Lardner had Arthur Treacher in mind
when he wrote it, Elder says.)

> I feel just like poor Hamo-let
> Who said, "To be or not to?"
> To kill oneself is wrong, and yet
> I b'lieve I've almost got to.
> The girl I love is so unkind!
> When I am gone, she'll rue it.
> So I will die if I can find
> A pleasant way to do it.

Refrain:
> But cyanide, it gripes inside;
> Bichloride blights the liver;
> And I am told one catches cold
> When one jumps in the river.
> To cut my throat would stain my coat
> And make my valet furious.
> Death beckons me, but it must be
> A death that ain't injurious.

2nd Refrain:
> A shot would make my eardrums ache
> And wake my niece, who's teething;
> A rope would wreck my classic neck

And interfere with breathing;
I can't take gas because, alas,
The odor's unendurable.
O Lord above, please tell me of
A death that ain't incurable.

Two of four sketches Lardner wrote for Flo
Ziegfeld's 1922 Follies were used, "Rip Van
Winkle, Jr." and "The Bull Pen," with Will
Rogers in the latter as one of three baseball
players. A 1927 collaboration with Robert Sherwood brought out an adaptation of Lardner's
story. "The Love Nest," which ran a mere
twenty-three performances.

Lardner's story, "Hurry Kane" underwent a
metamorphosis and his protagonist, a bone-headed
baseball pitcher devoid of scruples and common
sense, emerged as a baseball hero who saved the
game from gamblers in *Elmer the Great* (1928),
the play that Ring Lardner and George M. Cohan
wrote. Originally entitled *Fast Company, Elmer
the Great* opened in Boston, got a fair Chicago reception, and ran forty performances in New York
before expiring. Its stage failure did not prevent it
later becoming a film, first as *Fast Company,* star-
ring Jack Oakie, then as *Elmer the Great,* with
Joe. E. Brown.

With George Kaufman, Lardner reworked
his story, "Some Like Them Cold" to create *June
Moon* (1929). The story was hardly recognizable
in the play, but Lardner worked hard at writing
and rewriting, heeding Kaufman's suggestions.
After a shaky opening in Atlantic City required
more changes, the show moved on to success in
Washington. On October 9, 1929, *June Moon*
opened in New York City at the Broadhurst

Theater. It was a smash hit, ran 273 performances, and then enjoyed a good road trip.[8]
Ironically, the long-awaited success set Lardner on
a drinking bout which ended in the familiar pattern—drinking to illness to hospital stay to despair.

His last Broadway try was with Ziegfeld's
1930 attempt to produce *Smiles*. Vincent Youmans wrote the music, but his erratic behavior,
Ziegfeld's garrulous telegrams, and the egotistical
temperaments of the stars (Mildred Miller, Fred
and Adele Astaire) left Lardner in utter confusion
about what type of song was wanted for whom.
After Youmans had sung a tune to Lardner over
long distance, expecting him to supply the lyrics,
Lardner remarked that he respected Youmans "as
a composer [but] I would never recommend him to
Gatti-Casazza as a thrush." (Gatti-Casazza was at
that time General Manager of the Metropolitan
Opera in New York City.) All or part of six
Lardner lyrics were in *Smiles* when it opened
November 16, 1930, for a short Broadway run—
sixty performances. The chaotic time marked the
end of Lardner's Broadway aspiration.

Like baseball, music often figures in Lardner's work, frequently in parody, in characters who are song writers, and in various allusions
which show Lardner's knowledge not only of
popular songs, but of opera singers, plots, and
arias. "Carmen" (1916), one of the five Gullible
stories, recounts the events when the Gullibles and
the Hatches decide to go to a "musical show"
called *Carmen,* music by George S. Busy. Out of
their element altogether, the two husbands garble
the plot and make a general display of ignorance.
The wives strive to give the appearance of enjoy-
ing the music and of understanding the subtleties.

Gullible confuses the singers' names as well as the composer's, George S. Busy for Georges Bizet—"Marratory, Alda, Geneieve Farr'r that was in the movies a w'ile till they found out she could sing, and some fella they called Daddy, but I don't know his real name." In spite of Gullible's ineptness, Lardner is in fact quite accurate about the cast of *Carmen*. Ronald Davis in *Opera in Chicago* gives the dates and casts for opera in that city. In the 1915–1916 season (concurrent with the writing and publishing of Lardner's story, "Carmen") the first production of *Carmen* was on December 3, 1915, with Cleafonte Campanini conducting. Although the opera was presented eight more times that season, Frances Alda appeared only once; thus, the cast Lardner cites was apparently the December 3, 1915, performance: Don José was sung by Lucien Muratore ("Marratory"); Escamillo by Hector Dufranne ("Daddy," apparently to Gullible); Carmen by Geraldine (not Geneieve) Farrar; and Micaela by Frances Alda.

Lardner's familiarity with opera was far from casual (although Elder said it appalled him and Yardley declared he detested it), and his naming the contemporary singers who were associated with the *Carmen* roles indicates his care for accurate detail. As he did in other pieces, Lardner could and did put the right singer in the right role.

The conductor is "a Lilliputian with a match in his hand" (their seats were in the balcony) and Gullible's rehash of the plot (gleaned from a libretto Hatch picked up off the floor) rivals Richard Armour's *Twisted Tales from Shakespeare*. The burlesque of the opera comprises a third of the story and shows that Lardner

knew far more than a mere plot synopsis. The famous card scene, for example, is reported in Gullible's characteristic diction but with Lardner's skill
and insight. "So w'ile they're flatterin' each other
back and forth, a couple o' the girls is monkeyin'
with the pasteboards and tellin' their fortune, and
one o' them turns up a two-spot and that's a sign
they're goin' to sing a duet. So it comes true and
then Geneieve horns into the game and they play
three-handed rummy, singin' all the w'ile to
bother each other, but finally the fellas that's run-
nin' the picnic says it's time for the fat man's one-
legged race and everybody goes offen the stage."
In Bizet's opera, the card scene appears in Act 3
and through the turning of the cards, Carmen
learns of her own impending death.

Exposure to culture accomplishes little:
Gullible and Hatch remain unimpressed by the
performance and Mrs. Hatch exploits the occasion. She "buzzed all the way home, and she was
scared to death that the motorman wouldn't know
where sh'd been spendin' the evenin'. And if there
was anybody in the car besides me that knowed
Carmen it must of been a joke to them hearin' her
chatter."

Another of Lardner's stories intricately involved with music is "Rhythm" (1926). The narrator asks the reader to judge Harry Hart, a
songwriter presented in the four sections of the
story. First, the reader overhears a conversation at
the Friar's Club between Hart and Sam Rose, a
lyricist. Next, the narrator presents a past event, a
party at Gene Buck's (a lyricist and a friend of
Lardner's) where Hart plays other composers'
tunes claiming them as his own. The third section
goes farther into the past to report Hart's engage-

ment to Rita Marlow, the success of his musical
hit *Upsy Daisy,* and his rise to fame when Spencer
Deal publishes "Harry Hart, Harbinger" in
Webster's Weekly calling Hart "the pioneer in a
new American jazz . . . his rhythm would revolu-
tionize our music."

The climax of this third section occurs at
Peggy Leach's Sunday afternoon salon when Deal
announces that Hart "was at work on a 'blue'
symphony that would make George Gershwin's
ultra rhythms and near dissonants sound like the
doxology." Hart, haughty and rude to the guests,
plays the prima donna. The section ends with
Hart discarding Rita in favor of more socially useful women. The final section covers the reviews of
Hart's symphony which impressed critics less than
the compositions of Gershwin and Deems Taylor,
his return to producing mundane songs (stolen
tunes) with Benny Kane, and his reconciliation
with Rita.

"Rhythm" looks like an ordinary plot about
inflated and fallen pride (both Elder and Yardley
call the story an attack on pretentiousness), but it
is also an impressive glimpse into Lardner's ability
to introduce another level through musical allusions. The musical detail of these allusions escapes
some readers as the baseball detail in the Jack
Keefe stories escapes others. Nevertheless, a careful look at these musical references shows much
about Lardner's knowledge and much about music
in the twenties.

In part, "Rhythm" is about George Gershwin, *Rhapsody in Blue,* and ultra-sophisticated
jazz. On February 12, 1924, at 3 P.M. in
New York City's Aeolian Hall, Paul Whiteman
presented his carefully publicized and patronized

concert, "An Experiment in Modern Music."
Twenty-odd selections made up the eleven seg-
ments of a program that did not really live up to
Whiteman's claim of experiment until next-to-the-
last number. George Gershwin came to the piano
and Ross Gorman (who in rehearsal had, for
amusement, transformed Gershwin's opening
seventeen-note scalar run into the now familiar
human-tone glissando), Whiteman's virtuoso
clarinetist played the opening measures of *Rhapsody in Blue,* orchestrated by Frede Grofe. The
audience response was sensational. "When the
Rhapsody ended, there were several seconds of
silence and then all hell broke loose. A crescendo
of tumultous applause and enthusiastic cries swept
the house."[9] Gershwin had, as they said, brought
jazz out of the kitchen; he clearly was enthroned
as a dominant musical figure in the twenties.

The silliness of Harry Hart's extreme experi-
mentation (trying to out-Gershwin Gershwin), as
we shall see, is no worse than his return to his
normally successful song-writing practices—putting his rhythms to someone else's tunes while
Benny Kane changes someone else's words.
Pretentiousness, in other words, is hardly worse
than dishonesty.

Elder and Yardley insist that Lardner's
musical interests centered in popular songs, especially "coon songs" his friend Bert Williams sang
and romantic songs of Broadway appeal. That
assessment is true; however, when they insist with
equal vigor that Lardner was bored by symphonies
and appalled by opera, they overstate the case a
bit. Being bored and appalled by an art form does
not usually result in one's acquiring much information about that form. The musical allusions

in "Rhythm" demonstrate that Lardner's
knowledge was neither commonplace nor casual;
furthermore, a close examination of this story
should alert readers to the care with which
Lardner used musical allusions throughout his
writing.

The Broadway shows and popular songs that
Harry Hart has written include his most recent
hits *Upsy Daisy; Yes, Yes Eulalie* (with the smash
tune "Catch Me"); and *Lottie*. Sam Rose, his
second lyricist, wrote the words for *Nora's Nighty,
Sheila's Shirt*. Other popular songs are mentioned—"Arcady," "Marchete," "Buzz Around,"
and "Yes Sir, That's My Baby." The musicians
besides Hart and Rose are Benny Kane and
Spencer Deal. Snappy, catchy song titles and ordinary names of people contrast sharply with the
more stately names and titles of the three
composers and operas alluded to: Ponchielli's *La
Gioconda,* Donizetti's *Linda di Chamounix,* and
Verdi's *Aïda.*

When Hart's lyricist, Benny Kane, played
Hart's new tune for his wife, she knew Hart had
stolen it from some opera—"she thought it was
'Gioconda,' but she wasn't sure." Confronted with
the charge, Hart merely says it wasn't *Gioconda,*
but Donizetti's *Linda di Chamounix,* and twits
Kane for his attack of ethics. Hart's explanation
denigrates the audience and underscores his brashness. Admitting that he is a tune thief, Hart jus-
tifies his practice. "Well, how many of the dumb-
bells that goes to our shows has ever heard 'Linda
di Chamounix' or ever will hear it? When I put
the melody in our troupe I'm doing a million
people a favor; I'm giving them a chance to hear a
beautiful piece of music that they wouldn't never

hear otherwise. Not only that, but they'll hear it at
its best because I've improved it."

   Linda de Chamounix was first produced in
1842 and followed Donizetti's sensational *Lucia di
Lammermoor* of 1835. Neither opera had tunes
that needed Hart's improvements. Since *Linda di
Chamounix* was not in the Chicago Opera repertory, Lardner could not have seen a production
there. (The first performance at the Metropolitan
Opera was March 1, 1933. *Linda* was Galli-
Curci's first opera and it was a role sung by Patti
and later by Lily Pons.) Lardner does not hint
precisely which "pretty tune" Hart stole and made
into his "Donizetti number," but a reasonable
guess is Linda's Act I aria, "O, luce di quest'
anima," long a favorite concert piece.

   Even more involved is Lardner's use of a tune
from *Aïda*.

"Have you got any new tunes?"

"New?" Hart laughed. "I'm dirty with them." He sat
down at the piano. "Get this rhythm number. If it ain't
a smash, I'm Gatti-Casazza!"

He played it, beautifully, first in F sharp—a catchy refrain that seemed to be waltz time in the right hand and
two-four in the left.

"It's pretty down here, too," he said, and played it
again, just as surely, in B natural, a key whose mere
mention is henbane to the average pianist.

"A wow!" enthused Sam Rose. "What is it?"

"Don't you know?"

"The Volga Boat Song."

"No," said Hart. It's part of Aïda's number when she
finds out the fella is going to war. And nobody that

comes to our shows will spot it except maybe Deems
Taylor and Alma Gluck."

"It's so pretty," said Sam, "that it's a wonder it never
got popular."

"The answer is that Verdi didn't know rhythm," said
Hart.

Hart was hardly the equal of Gatti-Casazza
the Metropolitan's General Manager from 1908
until 1935. One must concede, however, that
Hart's piano playing agility is considerable since
the keys of F sharp and B natural are both difficult signatures, and probably equal henbanes to a
pianist. Quite clearly, Hart takes his Verdi tune
from Act I, scene i. Amneris sings the famous "Ri-
torna Vincitor," urging Radames' safe and victo-
rious return from battle. Then Aïda, left alone on
the stage, sings the famous aria which ends with
the prayer, "Numi, pieta." This portion does have
a fair amount of triplets for the soprano set against
two or four in the accompaniment, much like
Lardner's description, "waltz time in the right
hand and two-four in the left." Sam Rose's
wondering why the tune never got popular is
rivaled in absurdity only by Hart's explanation—
"Verdi didn't know rhythm."

Few in the audience are expected to recognize
the stolen tune, but Hart does mention two
interesting exceptions, Deems Taylor and Alma
Gluck. Taylor's opera *The King's Henchman* was
part of the Metropolitan repertory in 1926–1927
season and Taylor himself was the music critic for
the New York *World*. Alma Gluck sang at the
Metropolitan from 1909 until 1912 and then left
opera for a successful concert career with her vio-

linist husband, Efraim Zimbalist. Taylor and
Gluck would indeed have recognized Hart's Verdi
and Donizetti tunes.

Other musical allusions are numerous. After
Spencer Deal announced Hart's work on the
"blue" symphony, Hart insults Signor Parelli,
"one of the Metropolitan conductors," by saying
"Well, if I ever write an opera, I'll conduct it
myself, or at least I won't take no chance of having
it ruined by a foreigner." Hart then jostles Roy
Lattimer off the piano bench and plays for two
hours. The narrator does not name the pieces that
Hart performed, but he did not "play anything by
Kern, Gershwin, Stephen Jones, or Isham Jones,
Samuels, Youmans, Friml, Stamper, Tours,
Berlin, Tierney, Hubbell, Hein, or Gitz-Rice."
Lardner's catalog includes the leading song writers
of the twenties, a company of stiff competition for
Harry Hart, tune thief.

Hart's "blue" symphony hardly took the
musical world by storm and like Jack Keefe,
he shifts the blame for failure to prejudices.
"Gershwin was ahead of me and of course Taylor
has friends on the paper." Unlike Gershwin,
whose classical pieces of the twenties—*Rhapsody
in Blue* (1924), *Prelude for Piano* (1926), and *An
American in Paris* (1928)—stood along side his
successful Broadway musicals—*Lady Be Good*
(1924), *Song of the Flame* and *Tip Toes* (1925),
Oh, Kay (1926), *Rosalie* (1928), *Show Girl*
(1929)—Hart cannot make the transition. Engaged by Conrad Green (that semi-literate
producer) to write music for a new show, Hart
chooses Spencer Deal as lyricist. What they come
up with is "a score that required a new signature

at the beginning of each bar, and as much chance
of being unriddled, let alone sung, by chorus girls
as a pandect on biotaxy by Ernest Boyd."

A failure at experiment in modern music
(classical and popular), Hart rejoins his old
lyricist, Benny Kane, whose wife has let lean times
dull her ethics. Hart and Kane resume their tune
and lyric thievery, anticipating more hit shows like
Upsy Daisy.

Just a month before he died, Lardner's radio
column for the *New Yorker* was entitled, "The
Perfect Radio Program" (August 26, 1933). Here
he assigned comedians and musicians (popular and
operatic) in a rapid-fire order to his ideal
program, alloting each skimpy time, one to four
minutes. Popular musicians included Bing Crosby,
Guy Lombardo, Benny Goodman, Fanny Brice,
Ed Wynn, Fred Allen, and George Burns and
Gracie Allen.

Two opera stars were given slots and their
appearance is a final word about Lardner's
considerable muscial knowledge. "Rosa Ponselle,
singing an aria from the opera 'Norma.' (Two
minutes and a half.)" The 1927–1928
Metropolitan Opera season presented the long-
awaited appearance of Rosa Ponselle in *Norma,*
on November 16, 1927. Critics said of her singing
the aria from *Norma,* the "Casta Diva," a
"genuinely beautiful piece of singing." The other
opera star in Lardner's perfect program was "A
fellow named Lawrence Tibbett, singing in
English a song called 'Bendemeer's Stream,' or, in
Italian, the aria in 'Traviata' which Daddy sings
to the gal and which is virtually a complete history
of France up to the time the United States entered

the world war. (Two minutes.)" Tibbett did sing the role of Germont (Alfredo's "Daddy") in *La Traviata*; however, the famous "Di Provenza" aria covers a bit less than Lardner claims.

Quite obviously, Lardner was not always serious about opera and used aspects of it satirically and humorously. Nevertheless, he also used much of it with accuracy and skill. Lardner's love for baseball cooled considerably after the 1919 scandal, but his love for music never lessened even though he could not earn his living as he doubtless wished he could, as a songsmith.

7

A Natural

The last thirteen years of Ring Lardner's life were divided between an upswing of growing success, happiness, and creativity and a downturn of poor health, unhappiness, and diminishing work. Early success as a sports writer had spiraled his reputation and income. As a short story writer he attracted considerable attention; as a man, he was respected for his kindness, his innate generosity, and his morality.

Lardner's position in American letters rests primarily on the fiction, and somewhat on the nonsense plays, and the various magazine pieces he wrote from 1914 until his death in 1933. Not suited to actual productions, the nonsense plays are relatively unknown except to Lardner scholars, and most of the nonfiction has not been reprinted.[1] Except for those frequently anthologized—"Haircut," "Champion," "Some Like Them Cold," "The Golden Honeymoon," "The Love Nest"— most of his short stories are unfamiliar to students of American literature. Never ignored by his contemporaries and never neglected by later critics, Lardner nevertheless has not enjoyed a large literary following.

In the twenties, Scott Fitzgerald and Max Perkins frequently urged Lardner to undertake a long work on a serious topic. Fitzgerald was convinced that Lardner never realized his full talents; while Perkins praised Lardner's achievement in the short story, he too wanted the longer work. To their proddings, Lardner demurred, writing Perkins a typical refusal: "'Show business' has kept me so busy that I haven't even considered the novelette." As late as 1931, at a time when Lardner was far from well, Perkins wrote, "I wish you would take a year off from New York, and the theater, etc., and quietly do a novel!"[2]

That Lardner did not produce the long work Perkins and Fitzgerald encouraged may point to his limitations as a writer. The short story was his métier and, in spite of some evidence to the contrary, he valued his work and judged it with discretion. For example, when Scribner's brought out the uniform edition, Lardner wrote Perkins in 1925 asking that a set be sent to each of his brothers and sisters whose addresses were included. A 1927 letter to Perkins shows that Lardner did not think all his stories should be collected. "Cosmopolitan has enough stories, already printed or to be printed, to fill a book, but only about two of them are worth putting in a book. I'd rather wait until there are enough decent ones or until I've done something 'different.'"[3]

Lardner's big money came from his journalistic writing and from placing short stories in popular magazines like the *Saturday Evening Post, Cosmopolitan,* and *Redbook.* Max Perkins indicated once that *Scribner's Magazine* could not afford Lardner's prices. To a great extent, money determined what Lardner wrote and where he published.

In *My Family Remembered,* Ring Lardner, Jr. succinctly assesses Lardner's view of his own work, but that view, it must be remembered came after all from a humorist, a satirist, a cynic. "He

rarely had anything serious to say about his own
work. When he was in Boston in 1930 with a
Ziegfeld musical, a reporter asked him how he
came to write lyrics and Ring said, 'Someone gave
me a rhyming dictionary for Christmas once and I
couldn't exchange it for a tie.' ... But he was
part-way serious when he said he would rather do
almost anything than write short stories but had
no choice 'because I have four children and a wife
who has extravagant ideas about a garden.'"[4]
Jonathan Yardley quite rightly points to the em-
phasis on money in Lardner's career by quoting
Doctor Johnson in the frontispiece of his 1977
Lardner biography: "No man but a blockhead
ever wrote except for money."

Lardner came to a literary career through
mere chance and circumstance rather than with
burning ambition, and he certainly began to write
with less than a distinguished education. His
formal schooling did not match his self-education
through the experience of writing daily newspaper
columns well. He read from his youth on, keeping
up with contemporary writing but preferring
Russian literature, particularly Dostoyevsky;
above all *The Brothers Karamazov* was so much
his favorite novel that he read it over again every
few years.[5]

His favorite short story writer of all time was
Katherine Mansfield and he enjoyed reading
Gertrude Stein. Often he used literary allusions to
separate people and reveal their backgrounds as a
1925 letter to Fitzgerald shows Lardner's reading
habits and a nurse's lack of them. "I took 'Vanity
Fair' (Thackeray's, not Crowninshield's) to the
hospital with me and one day the nurse asked
what I was reading and I told her and she said, 'I

haven't read it yet. I've been busy making Christmas presents.'"[6]

Influenced particularly by Peter Finley Dunne and George Ade, Lardner was one of America's important humorists. Like Ade, his was a humor of disenchantment. What Bernard Duffey said about Ade applies equally to Lardner for they both "spoke for a growingly skeptical American wit, one that most readily found the stuff of laughter in the hardness of urban knowledge, in the cost of folly and the presumed hollowness of triumph."[7] George Ade readily responded with his familiar, "Oh, yeah?"; Lardner's counterpart was, of course, "What of it?"

Critical opinion about Lardner divided itself between an appreciative and vast newspaper reading public who read "In the Wake of the News" and later "Weekly Letter" with delight; and perhaps a more serious group of readers who valued his satiric short stories and nonsense plays. The publication of *How To Write Short Stories* (1924) was a turning point for Lardner since serious critics took that book seriously. Mencken had been an early champion, praising especially Lardner's keen ear for the minor peculiarities in his characters' speech. The twenties brought Lardner's books to the desks of reviewers on prestigious newspapers and journals and to the attention of prominent literary critics, some of whom praised aspects that others criticized. Over the years, "critical opinion of Lardner has ranged from those who describe him as a popular light humorist to those who praise him for his bitterly pessimistic criticism of American society."[8]

Lardner's technical skill has had its detractors. John Berryman saw his gift for mimicry, bur-

lesque, and parody but insisted that Lardner had
"no invention, little imagination, a very limited
sense of style, and almost no sense of structure."[9]
On the other hand, both Elder and Yardley praise
Lardner's ingenuity and quality of invention
which he developed and sharpened during his
newspaper writing days and perfected in his fiction. Skill is demanded, Elder notes, for a baseball
reporter "to be entertaining between games when
not very much is happening."[10] Lardner's trade-
mark was the non sequitur; he had the ability to
report accurately the way his characters talked and
thought; and above all he had the intelligence and
the timing, as Yardley said, "to determine what
went in and what stayed out, what was emphasized and what was underplayed."

Praise from some contemporaries was lavish,
albeit deserved. Perkins had sent a copy of Will
James's *Cowboys North and South* which Zelda
read aloud, Fitzgerald replied, "to spare my mind
and I love it—tho I think he learned the American
language from Ring rather from his own ear."[11]
After Perkins read "Haircut" he wrote Lardner,
"I can't shake it out of my mind;—in fact the im-
pression it made has deepened with time. There's
not a man alive who could have done better, that's
certain."[12] Returning from London, Perkins
reported to Lardner that he had seen Sir James
Barrie, who spoke with the greatest enthusiasm
about Lardner's work and said he read everything
of his that he saw. When *How To Write Short
Stories* was published, Mr. Scribner sent a copy to
Barrie and Perkins one to Galsworthy.

In his own time, Lardner was clearly judged
to be among the best of contemporary short story
writers. Bennett Cerf wished to include him in a

Modern Library book, *The Best Modern Stories: A 20th Century Anthology.* Harold Ober, the literary agent, described Cerf's project in a 1929 letter to Fitzgerald. Dependent on a story apiece from about twelve authors, Cerf had received permission to publish from Joseph Conrad, E. M. Forster, D. H. Lawrence, and Somerset Maugham. Cerf wanted, Ober wrote Fitzgerald, "a story by you and by Hemingway and one by Lardner. I should think it would be a good thing for you to have a story in this volume. You can see the quality of the volume when he told me that he did not think that Booth Tarkington was good enough to include. He tells me that he saw Mr. Arthur Scribner and he would not give him permission to use any of your stories. I judge he also refused to let them have stories by Hemingway and by Lardner."[13]

In mid-December, 1935, Sherwood Anderson wrote hastily and excitedly to Max Perkins about a new author, Evan Shipman, whose book, *Free for All,* Perkins had recently sent. The brief passage places Lardner in the first rank of American short story writers, at least from Anderson's point of view. "Dear Max Perkins: Excuse desk paper. I wanted to write a note to tell you that yesterday you gave me a grand thrill, the same sort I got when I first read a Hemingway, a Ring Lardner, a Bill Faulkner story. This Evan Shipman, he's got it."[14]

Persistently and correctly, critics have praised Lardner's unerring use of the vernacular as the means of displaying the depressingly mundane mind of the "American boob." George Whicher judged Lardner's speciality to be "his ability to report with seeming unconsciousness the appalling

mediocrity and vanity of the middle-class soul."[15]
Charles Poore called him "one of the most
penetrating of our short-story writers, one of the
funniest of our humorists, one of the most inexora-
ble of our moralists."[16] C. Hugh Holman
described him as a superb master of the spoken
language who "created a long line of characters
whose idiom was recorded with great precision,
while the frequently vain and empty man behind
the words stood forth sharply revealed."[17]

While critics today do not accept the view of
Lardner as a misanthrope, the "triangle of hate"
theory propounded chiefly by Clifton Fadiman and
Ludwig Lewisohn, no careful reader can deny the
note of pessimism, often of utter despair in his
writing. His constant battle with alcohol brought
problems, guilt, and broken health. World War I,
the Jazz Age, and Prohibition shattered the idyllic
past. The American push to materialism gave little
time for people to be interested in other people or
in their own inner development. It was a world to
accommodate the likes of the Gullibles, the
Grosses, and the Finches. John Berryman saw in
Lardner's nonsense plays the trait that penetrates
and indeed dominates all of his serious work. "But
surely what they [the nonsense plays] are about is
the failure of communication in the modern world,
and especially in the modern American world,
which is all Lardner cared about."[18] Howard W.
Webb, one of Lardner's best critics, echoes
Berryman when he says that Lardner's personal
world, "like his fictional world, was one in which
people did not listen and would not understand."[19]
The contemporary poet, Josephine Jacobsen,
begins her poem "Instances of Communication"
with a line Lardner would have ascribed to

readily: "Almost nothing concerns me but communication."

The middle class of the 1920s, Lardner's
primary subject matter, were a rootless bunch,
represented in his fiction by many characters like
the Keefes, Gullibles, Grosses, Finches. They all
lack, Donald Elder has noted, any fixed place in
society, any code of conduct. Symptomatic of the
breaking up of American life in the twenties, they
are transient, always on trains, in hotels, at race
tracks. Only skirting the society they can not join,
they are incapable of real pleasure. "As the
twenties progressed, Lardner's disillusionment
with America took a bolder and harsher fictional
shape."[20] The harsher view came, Maxwell
Geismar says, from his "extraordinary sense of in-
nocence about life—and a deep morality—that
were violated by the materialistic aspects of
American society and of mature life which the rest
of us more or less take for granted. It was this deep
feeling for the purity of life that led to the bitterness
and despair beneath his satire."[21]

Lardner's characters at times face their
ghosts, the truth about their flawed natures, their
petty and self-serving ways; but the insight is always too brief to effect substantial change, doubtless because Lardner did not find real or fictional
people capable of making things much better.
"For the foolish, as for the mad, Lardner offered
little solace. For the man of decency and common
sense he offered none at all."[22] His bleak picture
of men and manners was not relieved by a promise
from former days, picnics with strawberries and
courtships at arm's length. No matter how
Lardner's subject matter changed, "he never lost

his skill with language, his comic sense of incongruity, or his pessimistic despair."[23]

In 1924, Edmund Wilson speculated, "Will Mr. Lardner, then, go on to his *Huckleberry Finn*? Or has he already told all he knows? . . . His popular vein is about worked out; and he has always been too much of an artist to make the biggest kind of success as a clown; his books have never sold so well as Stephen Leacock's or Irvin Cobb's. When Lewis himself, in his earlier phase as a humorist for the *Saturday Evening Post,* took a chance and composed in *Main Street* his satire upon its readers, he received unexpected support. It turned out that there were thousands of people who were ready to hear what he wanted to say. What bell might not Lardner ring if he set out to give us the works?"[24]

Lardner never did "give us the works," but as a spokesman of the twenties he showed how many people lived, bearing and displaying their foibles, pettiness, misguided ambition, misplaced values. He was a superb humorist, an effective satirist, and a gifted short story writer. His *Huckleberry Finn* did not come, but readers are much in his debt for a great deal of entertainment and some excellent writing.

In his *Memories,* Sherwood Anderson found that writing down facts about his life was a difficult task because, he said, "I am by nature a story teller. No one taught me. Like such men as Erskine Caldwell, Ring Lardner and other men I've known I'm a natural."[25] So was Ring Lardner.

Notes

1. The Only Quiet Man in New York

1. Donald Elder, *Ring Lardner, A Biography* (Garden City, New York: Doubleday & Company, 1956), p. 90. Elder's biography remains the primary source of anecdotes about Lardner and this chapter bases such anecdotes on Elder unless otherwise noted.
2. Ring Lardner, Jr., *The Lardners: My Family Remembered* (New York: Harper & Row, 1976), p. 65.
3. Ibid., p. 148.
4. Jonathan Yardley, *Ring, A Biography of Ring Lardner* (New York: Random House, 1977), p. 255.
5. Donald Elder, *Ring Lardner,* p. 181.
6. Jonathan Yardley, *Ring,* p. 262.
7. Andrew Turnbull, ed., *The Letters of F. Scott Fitzgerald* (New York: Charles Scribner's Sons, 1963), p. 230.
8. Ring Lardner, Jr., *My Family Remembered,* pp. 191–192.
9. In a letter Turnbull dates circa February 25, 1926, Fitzgerald wrote Perkins, "I'm glad you got Hemingway. I saw him for a day in Paris on his return and he thought you were great. I've brought you two successes (Ring and Tom Boyd) and two failures (_ _ _ _ and_ _ _ _). Andrew Turnbull. ed., *Letters of Scott Fitzgerald,* p. 200.
10. Edmund Wilson, "Ring Lardner's American Characters" in *Literary Chronical: 1920–1950*

(Garden City, New York: Doubleday Anchor Books, 1952), p. 40.

11. Andrew Turnbull, ed., *Letters of Scott Fitzgerald*, pp. 181–182.

12. A Scott Berg, *Max Perkins, Editor of Genius* (New York: E. P. Dutton, 1978), p. 78.

13. Robert E. Spiller, et al., eds., *Literary History of the United States*, 3rd ed. rev. (London: The MacMillan Company, 1963), p. 1234.

14. Walton Patrick, *Ring Lardner* (New York: Twayne Publishers, 1963), pp. 121–130, discusses Lardner's uncollected stories.

15. Andrew Turnbull, ed., *Letters of Scott Fitzgerald*, p. 279.

16. Ring Lardner, Jr., *My Family Remembered*, p. 269.

2. COMMON AMERICAN

1. Hemingway's battle with unprintable words in *A Farewell to Arms* is recounted in A. Scott Berg, *Max Perkins: Editor of Genius* (New York: E. P. Dutton, 1978), pp. 141–142. Carroll Grimes has analyzed Hemingway's 1934 *Esquire* article in "Hemingway's 'Defense of Dirty Words': A Reconsideration," *Fitzgerald/Hemingway Annual* (1975), pp. 217–227.

2. Carroll Grimes, "Hemingway's 'Defense of Dirty Words,'" p. 221.

3. Ibid., p. 223.

4. Mary Austin, "Sex in American Literature," *Bookman*, LVII (June 1923), 391.

5. H. L. Mencken, Review of *How To Write Short Stories*, *American Mercury*, 2 (1924), 376.

6. Donald Elder, *Ring Lardner, A Biography* (Garden City, New York: Doubleday, 1956), p. 121.

7. Charles S. Holmes, "Ring Lardner: Reluctant Artist," in *A Question of Quality, Popularity and*

Value in Modern Creative Writing, ed., Louis
Filler (Bowling Green, Ohio: Bowling Green
University Popular Press, 1976), pp. 38–39.

8. Jonathan Yardley, *Ring, A Biography of Ring
Lardner* (New York: Random House, 1977), p.
189.

9. Howard W. Webb, Jr., "The Development of a
Style: The Lardner Idiom," *American Quarterly,*
12 (Winter 1960), 482.

10. Delmore Schwartz, "Ring Lardner: Highbrow in
Hiding, "*Reporter,* XV, (9 August 1956), 52–54.

11. Wayne C. Booth, *The Rhetoric of Fiction*
(Chicago: University of Chicago Press, 1961), p.
397.

12. Edmund Wilson, *The Twenties,* ed. Leon Edel
(New York: Farrar, Straus, and Giroux, 1975),
p. 187.

13. Samuel Richardson, *Clarissa* (1748; rpt. New
York: The Modern Library, 1950), p. 67.

14. Max J. Herzberg, *The Reader's Encyclopedia of
American Literature* (New York: Thomas Y.
Crowell Company, 1962), p. 218.

15. Jonathan Yardley, *Ring,* pp. 221–222.

16. Josephine Herbst, Introd., *Gullible's Travels,
Etc.,* by Ring Lardner (Chicago: University of
Chicago Press, 1965), p. xiii.

17. Maxwell Geismar, *Ring Lardner and the Portrait
of Folly* (New York: Thomas Y. Crowell, 1972),
p. 88.

18. Donald Elder, *Ring Lardner,* p. 285.

19. Louis Hasley, "Ring Lardner: The Ashes of
Idealism," *Arizona Quarterly,* 26 (1970), 224.

20. Jonathan Yardley, *Ring,* p. 272.

3. HARPIES AND GOLD DIGGERS

1. Jonathan Yardley, *Ring, A Biography of Ring
Lardner* (New York: Random House, 1977), p.
290.

2. Maxwell Geismar, *Ring Lardner and the Portrait of Folly* (New York: Thomas Y. Crowell, 1972), p. 95.
3. Donald Elder, *Ring Lardner, A Biography* (Garden City, New York: Doubleday & Company, 1956), p. 144.

4. PLAYERS, CHEATS, SPOIL SPORTS

1. In a roadhouse after the second game of the 1919 World Series, Lardner and three fellow journalists expressed their sentiments in new lyrics for the tune, "I'm Forever Blowing Bubbles."

> I'm forever blowing ball games
> Pretty ball games in the air.
> I come from Chi.,
> I hardly try,
> Just go to bat and fade and die.
> Fortune's coming my way,
> That's why I don't care.
> I'm forever blowing ball games,
> For the gamblers treat me fair.

See Jonathan Yardley, *Ring, A Biography of Ring Lardner* (New York: Random House, 1977), p. 214f. for a full discussion.
2. The composition of the baseball itself changed considerably in 1911 when a cork center replaced the rubber core. More hitting and longer games resulted. In 1920, the new ball ushered in the homerun era. As late as 1930, Lardner still rued the change this ball created in a *New Yorker* article, "Br'er Rabbit Ball" (13 September 1930).
3. Virginia Woolf, *The Moment and Other Essays* (New York and London: Harcourt Brace Jovanovich, 1974), p. 123.
4. Ibid.
5. H. L. Mencken, Review of *How To Write Short Stories, American Mercury,* 8 (1924), 376.

6. Donald Elder, *Ring Lardner, A Biography* (Garden City, New York: Doubleday and Company, 1956), p. 121.

7. Philip R. Roth, *The Great American Novel* (New York: Holt, Rinehart and Winston, 1973), p. 55.

8. The prototype for Jack Keefe may have been a White Sox player named Jack Gibbs who would not admit that he could not read or write. Sensing the man's weakness, Lardner began mumbling menus aloud and soon Jack Gibbs knew more to order than steak and baked potato or ham and eggs. Lardner was coerced into writing a letter to the man's wife and "Dear Myrt" bears some resemblance to Jack Keefe's letters to "Dear Al." Characteristically, Lardner disposed of the Jack Keefe origin question in the preface to *You Know Me Al*: "The original of Jack Keefe is not a ball player at all, but Jane Addams of Hull House, a former Follies girl."

9. Donald Elder, *Ring Lardner,* pp. 205–206. In "This Unsporting Life: The Baseball Fiction of Ring Lardner [*Markham Review,* II (February 1971), p. 27], Allan F. Stein takes a different view: "Lack of any intention on Lardner's part to present sports as an ordered context is readily apparent when we note first that the events on the field are often ludicrously far-fetched and, second, that Lardner sees no correlation between virtue, or even talent, and victory."

10. Johan Huizinga,*Homo Ludens,* translated by R. F. C. Hull (New York: Roy Publishers, 1950), p. 10.

11. One of Lardner's many verses points to the disparity between the ideal game and the real player.

> Players who jump for the dough,
> Bandits and crooks, every one.
> Baseball's a pleasure, you know.
> Players should play for the fun.

12. Jonathan Yardley, *Ring, A Biography of Ring*

Lardner (New York: Random House, 1977), p. 309.

13.   Johan Huizinga, *Homo Ludens,* p. 10.

14.   Roth treats the hero theme in *The Great American Novel,* p. 57. In describing the reaction of 1933 baseball enthusiasts to pitcher, Gil Gamesh, Roth writes, "And to the little kids of America, whose dads were on the dole, whose uncles were on the booze, and whose older brothers were on the bum, he was living, breathing example of that hero of American heroes, the he-man, a combination of Lindbergh, Tarzan, and (with his long, girlish lashes and brilliantined black hair) Rudolph Valentino: brave, brutish, and a lady-killer, and in possession of a sidearm fastball that according to Ripley's 'Believe It or Not' could pass clear through a batter's chest, come out his back, and still be traveling at 'major league speed.'"

15.   Elliott's negative attitude can be countered by many real players as Lardner's praise for Morris Rath shows. In the Chicago *Examiner* in August 1912, Lardner praised Rath as a man "who can be depended on to hold up his end, offensively and defensively." (See Yardley for a fuller quotation of the article, p. 36).

16.   Louis D. Rubin, Jr., "The Great American Joke," in *The Comic Imagination in American Literature,* ed., Louis D. Rubin, Jr. (New Brunswick: Rutgers University Press, 1973), p. 9.

17.   Johan Huizinga, *Homo Ludens,* p. 49.

5.   Humor of Disenchantment

1.   Constance Rourke, *American Humor* (1931; rpt. Garden City, New York: Doubleday & Company, 1953), p. 229.

2. Jonathan Yardley, *Ring, A Biography of Ring Lardner,* (New York: Random House, 1977), p. 340.

3. Brom Weber, "The Mode of Black Humor," in *The Comic Imagination in American Literature,* ed. Louis D. Rubin, Jr. (New Brunswick: Rutgers University Press, 1973), p. 362.

4. Ibid, p. 365.

5. H. L. Mencken, "A Humorist Shows His Teeth," *American Mercury,* 8 (June 1926), p. 255.

6. Clifton Fadiman, "Pitiless Satire," *Nation,* 128 (1 May 1929), p. 537.

7. Clifton Fadiman, "Ring Lardner and the Triangle of Hate," *Nation* 136 (22 March 1933), p. 315.

8. Ibid.

9. Walter Blair and Hamlin Hill, *America's Humor: From Poor Richard to Doonesbury* (New York: Oxford University Press, 1978), p. 413.

10. Brom Weber, "The Mode of Black Humor," p. 362.

11. Jonathan Yardley, *Ring,* pp. 254–255.

12. Jonas Spatz, "Ring Lardner: Not an Escape, but a Reflection," in *The Twenties,* ed. Warren French (Deland, Florida: Everett/Edwards, Inc., 1975), p. 103.

13. Ibid, p. 109.

14. Norris Yates, *The American Humorist, Conscience of the Twentieth Century* (Ames, Iowa: The Iowa State University Press, 1964), p. 188.

6. THE WOULD-BE SONGSMITH

1. Ring Lardner, Jr., *The Lardners: My Family Remembered* (New York: Harper & Row, 1976), p. 21.

2. Jonathan Yardley, *Ring, A Biography of Ring*

Lardner (New York: Random House, 1977), p. 101.

3. Ibid., p. 118.
4. Ibid., p. 129.
5. Ibid, p. 192.
6. Donald Elder, *Ring Lardner: A Biography* (Garden City, New York: Doubleday & Company, 1956), p. 261.
7. Ibid., p. 274–276.
8. Burt Shevelove did a television adaptation of *June Moon* which was staged in 1974 on the Public Television program, *Theater in America.* Successful adaptation, cast, and staging could not salvage a work totally linked to the twenties. See Jonathan Yardley, *Ring,* p. 337f. for a full discussion.
9. Charles Schwartz, *Gershwin, His Life and Music* (Indianapolis and New York: Bobbs-Merrill, 1973), p. 87.

7.   A NATURAL

1. Henry Morgan and Babette Rosmond, ed., *Shut Up, He Explained* (New York: Charles Scribner's Sons, 1962), contains nine of Lardner's nonsense plays and fourteen of the *New Yorker* "Over the Waves" radio columns. Matthew J. Bruccoli and Richard Layman, eds., *Some Champions, Sketches and Fiction by Ring Lardner* (New York: Charles Scribner's Sons. 1975), reprints seventeen articles and nine short stories.
2. Clifford Caruthers, ed., *Ring Around Max: The Correspondence of Ring Lardner and Max Perkins* (Dekalb, Illinois: Northern Illinois University Press, 1973), p. 152.
3. Ibid., p. 112.
4. Ring Lardner, Jr., *The Lardners: My Family*

Remembered (New York: Harper & Row, 1976), p. 175.

5. Ibid., p. 137.
6. Donald Elder, *Ring Lardner, A Biography* (Garden City, New York: Doubleday & Company, 1956), p. 197.
7. Bernard Duffey, "Humor, Chicago Style," in *The Comic Imagination in American Literature,* ed. Louis D. Rubin, Jr., (New Brunswick: Rutgers University Press, 1973), p. 213.
8. Forrest L. Ingram, "Fun at the Incinerating Plant: Lardner's Wry Waste Land," in *The Twenties,* ed. Warren French (Deland, Florida: Everett/Edwards, Inc., 1975), p. 112.
9. John Berryman, *The Freedom of the Poet,* preface by Robert Giroux (New York: Farrar, Straus and Giroux, 1976), p. 213.
10. Donald Elder, *Ring Lardner,* p. 94.
11. Andrew Turnbull, ed. *The Letters of F. Scott Fitzgerald* (New York: Charles Scribner's Sons, 1963), p. 17.
12. Clifford Caruthers, ed., *Ring Around Max,* p. 57.
13. Matthew J. Bruccoli, ed., *As Ever, Scott Fitzgerald, Letters Between F. Scott Fitzgerald and His Literary Agent Harold Ober, 1919–1940* (Philadelphia and New York: J. B. Lippincott Company, 1972), pp. 125–26.
14. Howard Mumford Jones, ed., *Letters of Sherwood Anderson* (Boston: Little, Brown and Company, 1953), pp. 338–339.
15. Max J. Herzberg, *The Reader's Encyclopedia of American Literature* (New York: Thomas Y. Crowell, 1962), p. 593.
16. Ibid.
17. C. Hugh Holman, "Anodyne for the Village Virus," in *The Comic Imagination in American Literature* (New Brunswick: Rutgers University Press, 1973), p. 250.

18. John Berryman, "The Case of Ring Lardner." p. 215.

19. Howard W. Webb., Jr., "The Meaning of Ring Lardner's Fiction: A Reevaluation," *American Literature* 31 (1960), p. 440.

20. Forrest L. Ingram, "Fun at the Incinerating Plant: Lardner's Wry Wasteland," p. 117.

21. Maxwell Geismer, *Ring Lardner and the Portrait of Folly* (New York: Thomas Y. Crowell, 1972), p. 86.

22. Howard W. Webb., Jr., "The Meaning of Ring Lardner's Fiction: A Reevaluation," p. 444.

23. C. Hugh Holman, "Anodyne for the Village Virus," p. 251.

24. Edmund Wilson, "Mr. Lardner's American Characters," in *A Literary Chronicle: 1920–1950* (New York: Doubleday Anchor Books, 1952), p. 40.

25. Ray Lewis White, ed., *Sherwood Anderson's Memoires: A Critical Edition* (Chapel Hill: University of North Carolina Press, 1969), p. 21.

Bibliography

1. WORKS BY RING LARDNER

Bib Ballads. Chicago: P. F. Volland & Company, 1915.

You Know Me Al. New York: George H. Doran Company, 1916.

Gullible's Travels, Etc. Indianapolis: Bobbs-Merrill, 1917.

My Four Weeks in France. Indianapolis: Bobbs-Merrill, 1918.

Treat 'Em Rough. Indianapolis: Bobbs-Merrill, 1918.

The Real Dope. Indianapolis: Bobbs-Merrill, 1919.

Own Your Own Home. Indianapolis: Bobbs-Merrill, 1919.

Regular Fellows I Have Met. Chicago: B. A. Wilmot, 1919.

The Young Immigrunts. Indianapolis: Bobbs-Merrill, 1920.

Symptoms of Being 35. Indianapolis: Bobbs-Merrill, 1921.

The Big Town. Indianapolis: Bobbs-Merrill, 1921.

Say It with Oil. New York: George H. Doran Company, 1923.

How to Write Short Stories. New York: Scribner's, 1924.

What of It? New York: Scribner's, 1925.

The Love Nest and Other Stories. New York: Scribner's, 1926.

The Story of a Wonder Man. New York: Scribner's, 1927.

Round Up. New York: Scribner's, 1929.

June Moon, with George S. Kaufman. New York: Scribner's 1930.

Lose with a Smile. New York: Scribner's, 1933.

First and Last, Edited by Gilbert Seldes. New York: Scribner's, 1934.

The Portable Lardner, edited by Gilbert Seldes. New York: Viking, 1946.

Shut Up, He Explained, edited by Babette Rosemond & Henry Morgan. New York: Scribner's, 1962.

The Best Short Stories of Ring Lardner, New York: Charles Scribner's Sons, 1957.

The Ring Lardner Reader, edited by Maxwell Geismar. New York: Scribner's, 1963.

Some Champions, edited by Matthew J. Bruccoli and Richard Layman. New York: Scribner's, 1976.

Ring Lardner's You Know Me Al. The Comic Strip Adventures of Jack Keefe, edited by Matthew J. Buccoli, New York: Harcourt Brace Jovanovich, 1979.

2. Books on Ring Lardner

Bruccoli, Matthew J., and Richard Layman, *Ring Lardner: A Descriptive Bibliography.* Pittsburgh: University of Pittsburgh Press, 1976.

Caruthers, Clifford, ed., *Ring Around Max: The Correspondence of Ring Lardner and Maxwell Perkins.* Dekalb, Illinois: Northern Illinois Press, 1973.

Elder, Donald, *Ring Lardner, A Biography.* Garden City, New York: Doubleday & Company, 1956.

Friedrich, Otto, *Ring Lardner.* Minneapolis: University of Minnesota Press, 1965.

Geismar, Maxwell, *Ring lardner and the Portrait of Folly.* New York: Thomas Y. Crowell, 1972.

Lardner, Ring Jr., *The Lardners: My Family Remembered.* New York: Harper & Row, 1976.

Yardley, Jonathan, *Ring, A Biography of Ring Lardner.* New York: Random House, 1977.

3.   ARTICLES ON RING LARDNER

Fadiman, Clifton, "Ring Lardner and the Triangle of Hate," *Nation,* 136 (22 March 1933), pp. 315–317.

Hasley, Louis, "Ring Lardner: The Ashes of Idealism," *Arizona Quarterly,* 26 (1970), pp. 319–322.

Holmes, Charles S., "Ring Lardner: Reluctant Artist." In *A Question of Quality, Popularity and Value in Modern Creative Writing.* Ed., Louis Filler, Bowling Green, Ohio: Bowling Green University Press, 1976, pp. 26–39.

Ingram, Forrest L. "Fun at the Incinerating Plant: Lardner's Wry Waste Land." In *The Twenties,* Ed., Warren French, Deland, Florida: Everett/Edwards, Inc., 1975, pp. 111–122.

Overton, Grant, "Ring W. Lardner's Bell Lettres." *Bookman,* LXII (1925), pp. 44–49.

Schwartz, Delmore, "Ring Lardner: Highbrow in Hiding." *Reporter,* XV (9 August 1956), pp. 52–54.

Smith, Leverett T., Jr., "The Diameter of Frank Chance's Diamond: Ring Lardner and Professional Sports." *Journal of Popular Culture, 6* (1972–73), pp. 133–56.

Spatz, Jones, "Ring Lardner: Not an Escape, but a Reflection." In *The Twenties.* Ed., Warren French, Deland, Florida: Everett/Edwards, Inc., 1975, pp. 101–110.

Stein, Allen F., "This Unsporting Life: The Baseball Fiction of Ring Lardner." *Markham Review,* 11 (1971), pp. 27–33.

Van Doren, Carl, "Beyond Grammar: Ring W. Lardner: Philologist among the Low-Brows," *Century,* CVI (1923), pp. 471–475.

Webb, Howard W., Jr., "The Development of a Style: The Lardner Idiom." *American Quarterly,* 12 (1960), pp. 482–492.

—————, "The Meaning of Ring Lardner's Fiction: A Reevaluation," *American Literature,* 31 (1960), pp. 434–445.

Wilson, Edmund, "Ring Lardner's American Characters." In *A Literary Chronicle: 1920–1950.* New York: Doubleday Anchor Books, 1956, pp. 37–44.

Yates, Norris, "The Isolated Man of Ring Lardner." In *The American Humorist: Conscience of the Twentieth Century.* Ames, Iowa: Iowa State University Press, 1964, pp. 165–193.

Index

MODERN LITERATURE MONOGRAPHS

In the same series